A History of Ottoman Poetry

Volume V: 1859-

THE E.J.W. GIBB MEMORIAL TRUST

A History of Ottoman Poetry

Volume V: 1859-

by E.J.W. Gibb

edited by

Edward G. Browne

Published by
THE E.J.W. GIBB MEMORIAL TRUST

Trustees: G. van Gelder, R. Gleave, C. Hillenbrand, H. Kennedy,
C. P. Melville, J. E. Montgomery, C. Woodhead
Secretary to the Trustees: P. R. Bligh

ISBN 978-0-90609-459-4

A CIP record for this book is available from the British Library

Further details of the E. J. Gibb Memorial Trust and its publications
are available at the Trust's website

www.gibbtrust.org

Printed and bound in Great Britain by
Marston Book Services Ltd, Oxfordshire

لِلّٰهِ كُنُوزٌ تَحْتَ ٱلْعَرْشِ مَفَاتِيحُهَا ٱلْسِنَةُ ٱلشُّعَرَاءِ

'God hath Treasuries aneath the Throne, the Keys whereof are the Tongues of the Poets.'

Hadís-i Sheríf.

EDITOR'S PREFACE.

The publication of this fifth volume of the *History of Ottoman Poetry* brings to a close the more essential part of the obligation which I undertook, at the wish of the mother and the widow of my late friend, Mr. E. J. W. Gibb, now nearly six years ago, to edit and secure the publication of the great and masterly work to which his too brief life was devoted. All that he wrote is now accessible to the Orientalist, the scholar, the student of literary history and the general reader. Whatever else may be alleged against the Ottoman Turks, it can never again be asserted by the candid and impartial reader that they are, or ever have been, since their first appearance on the stage of history in the thirteenth century, indifferent to literature. On the contrary, their fault in our own days, as it seems to me, is that they pay too much attention to literature, and expect from it (I speak now especially of the Modern School, with the protagonists of which the present volume deals) a salvation and regeneration which it cannot give. I have lately been looking with some attention into the mass of Turkish tracts and pamphlets which belonged to my late friend, and which were, with other literary materials, placed at my disposal by Mrs. E. J. W. Gibb, and nothing connected with them has impressed me more than the glorification of Turkish men of letters, especially of Ziyá Pasha, Shinásí, Kemál

Bey, Ekrem Bey, Mu'allim Nájí, 'Abdu'l-Ḥaqq Ḥámid Bey and others of the modern leaders of Ottoman literature, and the minute and almost meticulous criticisms of their works' which form so considerable a proportions of their contents. Again and again I have exclaimed to myself, "Would that the Turks had a literature comparable in value to those of the Arabs and Persians, and would that the Arabs and Persians had cultivated the art of literary criticism to a degree approaching that of the Ottoman Turks!"

It is, as I observed in the preface to the last volume (p. IX), a matter for profound regret that Gibb did not live to complete his account of the Modern School, with which he had a real sympathy, and for which he entertained a genuine admiration such as can hardly he found since his death outside Turkey. For this modern Ottoman literature, so far as Europe is concerned, is a kind of No Man's Land. The Orientalist by profession is disinclined to devote much time or labour to a literature which is not only quite modern but quasi-European, while the student of modern literary movements rarely possesses a sufficient knowledge of a language which, even in the simpler forms affected by the New School of Ottoman writers, remains more difficult than Arabic or Persian. Yet I begin to see (what I at first was disposed to doubt) than this modern Turkish literature has real value and merit; and, though I cannot myself hope to find leisure to exploit and appreciate it, I feel compelled to express an earnest hope that some other Turkish scholar may arise in Western Europe who will once and for all write its history and appraise its value.

Meanwhile I am still hopeful that Gibb's unfinished work may be completed by a very able Turkish man of letters, whose name I am not now at liberty to mention, and who has for some time been engaged on this work. Personally acquainted with most of the leading spirits of the New School, knowing English well and French still better, and animated by a genuine enthusiasm for his work, he has already surveyed a large portion of the field which Gibb did not live to cultivate. Yet, owing to the atmosphere of suspicion which now broods over Constantinople, and, in particular, the disfavour with which the political ideas of the "Young Turks" (to whose ranks most of the adherents of the New School of Literature belong) are regarded, his task is one of extreme difficulty, since even the works of Kemál Bey, the brightest light of that school while he lived, are banned by the Government and can hardly be seen in Constantinople. That this supplement will be finished in time I have little doubt, but the date of its completion remains so uncertain that is seemed to me best to complete Gibb's work without further delay by publishing the three chapters which he had written on the Modern School, together with the very full and careful Indices prepared by my friend and colleague Mr. R. A. Nicholson; to follow up this fifth volume with a sixth containing the Turkish texts of all the poems translated by Gibb; and to add later the seventh volume containing my Turkish collaborator's supplement, should this be finished and safely reach my hands. The sixth volume, containing the Turkish texts, is, I may add, complete in manuscript, and is now in the press, whence 112 pages of it have already been received in type, so that, if all goes well, it should be published next year. I am glad to say that ultimately, after many a laborious search through the manuscripts, printed books and note-books of my late friend, I have succeeded in recovering the original texts of all the translations contained in these volumes without exception.

My labours are therefore almost finished, and I am thankful that this is so, and that I have so nearly fulfilled the arduous duty which I undertook in December, 1901. My chief regret is that my late friend's mother did not live to see the accomplishment of the work in which she took so profound and affectionate an interest; my chief satisfaction, that I have been enabled to render to a great and single-minded scholar, whose friendship and sympathy I shall ever remember with gratitude and pleasure, that service which of all others he would have valued most.

August 1, 1907.   EDWARD G. BROWNE.

The Modern School of Ottoman Poetry, that in which the inspiring genius is no longer of the East, but of Western Europe, falls into two periods, the one of Preparation, the other of Accomplishment. The first begins in 1275 (1859) with the publication of Shinásí Efendi's Translations from the French poets; the second in 1296 (1879) with the appearance of Hámid Bey's Sahrá.

CHAPTER I.

The Dawn of a New Era.

1275—1296 (1859—1879).

We have now to tell the story of a great awakening. We have traced the course of poetic literature amongst the Ottoman Turks during five centuries and a half. We have learned how, throughout this long period, no voice has ever reached it from outside the narrow school where it was reared; how, Persian in its inception, Persian in substance it has remained down to the very end, driven back after a blind struggle to win free, baffled and helpless into the stagnant swamp of a dead culture. But now all is on the verge of change; Asia is on the point of giving place to Europe, and the tradition of ages is about to become a memory of the past. A voice from the Western world rings through the Orient skies like the trumpet-blast of Isráfíl; and lo, the muse of Turkey wakes from her death-like trance, and all the land is jubilant with life and song, for a new heaven and a new earth are made visible before the eyes of men. Now for the first time the ears of the people are opened to hear the speech of hill and valley, and their eyes unsealed to read the message of cloud and wave. The heavy fetters of secular tradition and convention are broken and cast away, and the poet finds himself at last a free man, free to seek his inspiration where he will, free to voice what is within him as he pleases.

The time is not yet come when it is possible fully and adequately to write the history of this Renascence. It has shot up and burst into glorious flower under our very eyes. We are too near to the great events that have brought it about to see these in true perspective; we cannot justly determine the relative importance of mighty changes effected while we are looking on. Moreover, we are still, perhaps, somewhat bewildered and dazed by the suddenness and completeness of the revolution, while even were it otherwise, the materials necessary to write a satisfactory account of its development are not yet available. The chief actors have been, as we shall see, more or less intimately concerned in the demand for political reform that has sprung up in the newly-awakened nation, and such accounts of them and their work as have yet appeared have been so mutilated and travestied by the jealous suspicion of the official censor as to be well nigh useless. I can, therefore, in the following chapters attempt no more than to outline the story of this great literary revival. To my successors must be left the task of producing the finished picture. More remote from the actual crisis and with ampler materials at their disposal, they will doubless be able not only to complete, but in many points to correct, my sketch.

It took the poets twenty years to attain that freedom of which I have spoken; and it is to the consideration of these twenty years during which the way was being prepared that I propose to devote the present chapter. During these two decades, from 1859 to 1879, the Europeanising movement initiated by Selím the Martyr and fostered by Mahmúd the Reformer and his son ʿAbd-ul-Mejíd, was becoming more than a mere external matter modifying the machinery of the administration and revolutionising the titles and costumes of the official world; it was striking its roots beneath the surface and beginning to exercise a powerful influence on the ideas and opinions of the more thoughtful of the people. The closer connection between Turkey and the Western states, brought about by political and commercial relations and the greater facilities of communication, naturally gave rise amongst intelligent Ottomans to a desire to form some acquaintance with a civilisation which enabled its possessors to achieve such brilliant success in so many diverse directions. This in its turn led men to undertake the study of the French language as the key to this new treasure-house of knowledge. And here we strike the true fountain head of all the development that follows. From the moment when the study of a Western language became general, transformation of the whole intellectual outlook was inevitable, and the only question remaining was when and how this should be accomplished.

The admission of the French language into the educational curriculum is the most revolutionary measure in the history of Ottoman culture. There has been nothing in any way resembling it in the past. This culture was, so to speak, born and reared in that of Persia; it did not adopt this latter, but grew up encompassed by it, unconscious of the existence of any other, so that it has sometimes been regarded, and not altogether unfairly, rather as a branch thereof than as an independent growth. The passage from one Persianist school to another has marked no revolution, but only the several steps in a process of development, or, if the word be preferred, of decline. The Romanticist revolt effected no radical or permanent change, but, for lack of guiding principle, soon spent itself, so that nothing was left but to fall back into the slough of Persianism. But now for the first time an entirely new world of ideas is opened out before the Ottoman mind; and with that genius for assimilation which, as we have so often noticed, is characteristic of the race, this new revelation is made part and parcel of the intellectual life, so that to the Turk of to-day the ghazels of ʿArif Hikmet and his school have come to seem as remote as do the poems of Gower or Occleve to ourselves.

Even when regarded from the literary side alone, the results of this measure have been stupendous. The hoary traditions of five hundred and fifty years, traditions which appeared ineradicably interwoven with the genius of the people, have been all reversed; what were formerly looked upon as merits are now held for faults, and what were once held for faults are now looked upon as merits. Not only have the canons of taste been revolutionised, but the whole conception of poetry has become absolutely changed. In the old time poetry was before all things an art, and whosoever knew and followed the rules of that art was called a poet; but he who would earn such title now must be the interpreter of the heart of man. In prose the change has been as complete and came earlier; while two entirely new forms of literature, the drama and the novel, the very names of which were unknown before, have been introduced and are now fully naturalised.

But the effects of the new education have been by no means confined to literature; the force of the revolution it produced has been felt all along the intellectual line, notably in science and in politics. Indeed, in the earlier years of ʿAbd-ul-Mejíd's reign, the few who then undertook the study of French did so almost exclusively for purposes of diplomacy or science, the literary possibilities it opened out being still, except in two memorable instances, practically ignored.

Hence it comes that the earlier historical and scientific treatises of Jevdet and Munîf Pashas, produced about the time of the accession of ʿAbd-ul-ʿAzíz, are written with modern knowledge but in the old style. In science, the new learning has transported Turkey from the middle ages to the present day; in politics, it has created the 'Young Turkey' party. This party, whose aims are liberty and progress, was called into existence by the same men who founded the new literature, and the stories of the two are closely linked together. So swiftly grew the demand for political reform which it evoked among the people, and so powerful did this become, that hardly a dozen years had passed ere the Sultan was forced to proclaim the Constitution. And although this Constitution is for the time being in abeyance, suppressed by the present reactionary régime, it is still theoretically the only lawful form of government in Turkey.

The new culture is spoken of by the Turks as 'gharbî' that is 'western' or 'occidental', and is contrasted with the 'sharqî', that is the 'eastern' or 'oriental'. As a matter of fact it is borrowed almost exclusively from France, the other western countries, England, Germany, Italy etc., having contributed little or nothing. Till about the middle of the nineteenth century the Turks who knew French were few and far between; but nowadays every person, man or woman, with any pretensions to education, knows something of the language and can speak and read it with more or less facility. An immense number of works, both literary and scientific, have of late years been translated from French into Turkish, thus enabling even those whose knowledge of the former language is defective to form some conception of 'western' ideas. French philosophers, French dramatists, French novelists, French poets, are now the models of the Turkish man of letters; indeed we might almost say that what Persia was

to the Ottomans of bygone years France is to their descendants
of to-day. The reason why France, or rather the French
language and literature, occupy this position of overwhelming
predominance may be found in the fact that French, being
the language of diplomacy, would naturally have the greatest
claim on officials such as were the first Turks who turned
their attention to things western. The French language would
thus get a start; the riches which, as was soon discovered, it
enshrines would commend it to the scholarly, while its great
utility as a lingua franca would readily be appreciated by all.

The first clear note of the revolution was not struck till
1859, but circumstances had for long been preparing the way
for the coming change. We have seen how poetry was in
a desperate plight, without compass and without rudder,
tossed to and fro between Persianism and Romanticism, in
sore need of some guiding light. The changes introduced
during the last fifty years had gradually accustomed men's
minds to the once distasteful idea of adopting anything
European; the suspicion born of ignorance had now in great
measure passed away. Then the foundation of the Enjumen-i
Dánish a few years earlier showed that there was some stir
in the intellectual world; the literary revival could not
therefore be far behind. Thus all was ready; the need was
great, the remedy at hand; nothing was wanting but the
man who could apply it.

Meanwhile he and his two lieutenants had been ·quietly
preparing themselves for their great work. These three
men — and their names are amongst the most illustrious in
the history of modern Turkey — are Shinásí Efendi, Kemál
Bey and Ziyá Pasha. It is primarily to these three that the
transformation of Ottoman literature and the creation of the
Young Turkey party alike are due. In the following chapters
we shall consider the work of each of these three reformers

in some detail, but a few words are necessary here to indicate the position in which they stand in relation to the new movement as a whole.

After studying in Paris, Shinásí returned to Constantinople, and there in the year 1859 he published a small volume of translations from various French poets. This was the first translation of a purely literary character ever made from a Western language into Turkish; and although it had little immediate effect, its appearance marks an epoch in Ottoman literature. By a strange coincidence this little book appeared in the same year in which died ʿArif Hikmet, the last poet of eminence of the Old School. Of much more immediate importance was the newspaper — the first non-official journal in Turkey — which Shinásí established in the following year, and in which he endeavoured to promote the great end he had in view. This end was briefly to approximate, as closely as might be, the intellectual life of Turkey to that of the Western nations. To effect this the first thing needful was obviously so to modify the literary language as to render it an adequate medium for the expression of the new and alien ideas which it was sought to naturalise. This was the chief part of Shinásí's work, and so successful was he here that his immediate heirs have been able from the foundations which he laid to elaborate a literary idiom little inferior in precision and directness to its western prototype. The remodelling of the language, however, was but a means to an end, so, while Shinásí devoted much thought and attention to all matters bearing thereon, he was careful to do what he could towards educating the people by publishing in his paper articles dealing with a great variety of scientific and social questions treated from a modern European point of view. Even politics were discussed with a certain degree of freedom, as under the easy-going régime

2

of those days writers enjoyed a considerable amount of liberty.

About two years after Shinásí had started his journalistic work he was joined by Námiq Kemál, then a young man of some twenty summers. This young man, who was destined to develop into one of the most brilliant writers Turkey has ever known, at once became the devoted disciple of Shinásí, whose aims and principles he adopted with enthusiasm, and whose ideals he eventually realised with a brilliancy and power far beyond anything which the master himself could ever have achieved. Indeed, when Kemál Bey died in 1888, at a comparatively early age, he left Ottoman prose, which he had found a chaotic welter, without rule or guiding principle, a powerful and delicate instrument capable of expressing with precision, force and grace the manifold complexity of modern thought.

While Shinásí was still maturing his schemes and Kemál was yet a lad in the provinces writing reams of verses in imitation of Nef'í and Fehím, the third of the group, Ziyá, then a secretary in the Palace, was independently and entirely on his own account, working in the same direction, translating French classics and constructing for himself a Turkish prose style modelled thereupon. Later on he joined forces with Shinásí and Kemál, and in 1867, when his quarrel with ʿAlí Pasha, the all-powerful vezir of ʿAbd-ul-ʿAzíz, made it inexpedient for him to remain in Constantinople, he accepted the invitation of the Egyptian prince, Mustafá Fázil Pasha, to join him in Europe, and along with Kemál and some others of the Young Turkey leaders he fled from his native country. The sojourn of these reformers in the West, which lasted till the death of ʿAlí Pasha some four years later, had naturally considerable influence in the development of their ideas both literary and political. Thus the aims of the party grew more precise; a definite demand for constitutional and responsible government took the place of the previous somewhat vague cry for reform, and a newspaper was established in which Kemál and Ziyá could not only give expression to their views and aspirations but continue to practise that art of the literary craftsman which to them was hardly less dear.

It is then to the labours of these three men that the creation of modern Ottoman prose is due. The application of the new principles to poetry does not come till later, not till Hámid Bey writes his Sahrá. It is with the appearance of this epoch-making booklet in 1879 that the true Modern School of Ottoman poetry begins. Shinásí, Kemál and Ziyá did indeed all write poetry, the last two, and particularly Kemál, being further poets of great merit and distinction. But partly because their chief aim was utilitarian, and partly because the bent of their genius lay rather towards prose than poetry, they did not bestow the same attention on the latter. Of the three, Kemál alone lived to profit by the change; for Shinásí was dead and Ziyá dragging out the last year or two of his life in virtual exile at Adana, when Hámid Bey inaugurated the new poetry of Turkey. The revelation came too late for them; but Kemál at once saw the potentialities it enshrined and applied himself to its cultivation with the splendid success that attended his every literary effort. It is because of his great success in the new poetry that I have in the following pages placed him amongst the poets of the true Modern School rather than alongside of his colleagues Shinásí and Ziyá.

The typical poetry of the twenty years under review finds its best exponent in Ziyá, Shinásí's work in verse being small in extent and of comparatively little moment. The distinguishing feature of this typical poetry is a combination of the modern spirit with the traditional machinery. The range of subject remains practically the same, the external form is wholly unaltered, but the point of view has changed. The poet looks at much the same things as did his ancestors, and speaks of them in much the same way, but he sees them in a new light and approaches them from a different direction. His knowledge, too, of things in general has grown more mature, so that if he still sometimes speaks about the Seven Spheres, he does so merely as a figure of speech, not because he is in any way ignorant of the nature of the solar system.

But although the more truly representative of its time and, as leading directly to the coming development, infinitely the more important, the poetry of this type is far from forming the bulk of the verse now produced. Most of the poets during these twenty years continued to work upon the lines of the Persianist reaction that had set in during the preceding Period. Nef'í is still on the whole the favourite model; but the poets are eclectic, and no single style is really predominant. The work they produced is often good, and, by the increased clearness and accuracy in thought which it occasionally displays, shows that the writers were not wholly insensible to the influences of the time; but its interest is little more than that of a survival, as the true voice of the age speaks elsewhere. None the less it is not without a certain pathos; for it is the swan-song of the old Oriental genius as it passes away before the all-conquering spirit of the west.

As I have already said, the study of French led to the introduction into Ottoman literature of two absolutely new forms, the novel and the drama. The first of these has no connection with poetry, and so perhaps lies somewhat outside our sphere; but as its appearance is an interesting event in the history of Turkish literature, it may be permissible to say a few passing words concerning it. Up till now there have been no true novels, nothing but some romances of the Arabian Nights type, the best known of which are the Qirq Vezír or Forty Vezirs, [1] the ꜤIbret-numá, or Monitor, of LámiꜤí, [2] and the Mukhayyalát, or Phantasms, of ꜤAlí ꜤAzíz. [3] In 1279 (1862) Yúsuf Kámil Pasha published in a very graceful though naturally old-fashioned style a translation of Fénelon's Télémaque. This was the first western work of fiction ever turned into Turkish. A few years later, when the number of those who knew the language increased, there began a rush of translations of novels of every description which continues unabated down to the present day, the result being that modern French fiction is now very fairly represented in Turkish. The Turks had of course no name for compositions of this kind, so they have adopted the French term and call a novel, whether original or translated, a 'román.' These French novels represent of course a manner of life foreign to Turkey; but it was not long before Ahmed Midhat Efendi, an eminent man of letters, conceived the idea of writing similar stories which should depict local life and manners. So in 1287 (1870-1) he began to publish a series of novelettes, under the collective title of Letá'if-i Riwáyát or Pleasant Tales,

[1] This collection of tales, the earliest Turkish version of which is at least as old as the time of Murád II, was translated and published by me in 1886, under the title of the 'History of the Forty Vezirs'. Nothing is known of the author or compiler, who is variously styled Sheykh-záde and Ahmed-i Misrí, i. e. Ahmed the Egyptian (or Cairene), both perhaps names of a single individual. The book is generally called Qirq Vezír Ta'ríkhi 'the History of the Forty Vezirs'; its correct title is Hikáyetu-ErbaꜤína Ṣabáḥan ve Mesà'an, "The Story of the Forty Morns and Eves."

[2] This is LámiꜤí the Suleymanic poet an account of whom is given in vol. iii, ch. 2.

[3] Giridli ꜤAlí ꜤAzíz, or ꜤAlí ꜤAzíz the Cretan, died in 1213 (1798-9). His Mukhayyalát consists of three 'Phantasms', one of which was translated and published by me in 1884, under the title of 'The Story of Jewád'.

which deal for the most part with Ottoman subjects, and in so doing he laid the foundation of the now flourishing branch of literature known as the 'millí román' or 'national novel'.

The drama, though at first exclusively and always more generally written in prose, was chosen by Hámid Bey as the form into which to cast some of the most noble of his poems, and therefore concerns us more closely than does the novel. The rise of the Ottoman drama proceeded naturally enough along the same lines as the rise of the Ottoman novel. In 1286 (1869—70), the celebrated Ahmed Vefíq Pasha published translations of three of Molière's comedies, namely 'George Dandin', 'Le Médecin malgré Lui', and 'Le Mariage Forcé'. In these translations, which are made with great ability and much spirit, the Pasha very cleverly adapted the scenes to Eastern life by here and there slightly modifying an incident or a phrase, and by re-christening the characters with Turkish or Levantine names. Thus George Dandin appears as a Greek with the name Yorgi Dandini; Sganarelle, the doctor by constraint, becomes the Turkish peasant ʿIwaz; while the Sganarelle of the forced marriage figures as ʿIwaz Agha. These three plays, which are entitled Yorgi Dandini, Zoraki Tabíb, and Zor Nikáhi respectively, were shortly afterwards produced upon the stage, their representation being the first true dramatic performance ever given in Turkish. The expenses of their production were defrayed by a subscription raised amongst those Turks interested in literature and culture; and notwithstanding the inevitable shortcomings of the Turco-Armenian troupe charged with the representation, the performances were very highly appreciated. Later on a permanent theatre for the representation of Turkish plays was established at Gedik Pasha in Stamboul, and this continued to be the chief temple of the Ottoman drama till its destruction by fire some years ago.

In 1288 (1871—2), two years after the appearance of
Vefíq Pasha's translations of Molière, Ebu-z-Ziyá Tevfíq
Bey, in collaboration with Kemál Bey (whose name, however,
did not appear) published the first original Turkish drama.
This was not a comedy like Vefíq's translations, but a
tragedy having for title Ejel-i Qazá or 'The Fated Doom'.

Ebu-z-Ziyá Tevfíq Bey, who is thus closely connected with
the introduction of the drama into Ottoman literature, has
frequently been mentioned in the course of our History.
Although not a poet, this scholarly and accomplished gentleman, with whom I have the pleasure of being personally
acquainted, has played so great a part in the new literary
movement and rendered such important services to its development, that any sketch thereof, however fragmentary, would be
grievously defective were his labours passed over unrecognised.
Early associated with Kemál Bey in journalistic work, Tevfíq
Bey soon became the intimate friend and warm admirer of that
great reformer, and about 1874—5, when Sultan ᶜAbd-ul-
ᶜAzíz, alarmed at the popularity of the latter, as shown by
the enthusiastic reception of his play 'The Fatherland',[1]
swept down upon the little group of pioneers and summarily
banished them to different corners of the Empire, Tevfíq
Bey was hurried off, an exile to the island of Rhodes. There
he employed his time in the compilation of a work which
has had a great and beneficial influence on the later literature.
This work, the first of its kind in Turkish, has often been
referred to in the preceding chapters. It is called Numúne-i
Edebiyyát-i ᶜOsmániyya or Specimens of Ottoman Literature,
and consists of a series of selected extracts from the works
of the most remarkable Ottoman prose writers, beginning
at the fifteenth century.[2] These selections have been care-

[1] Watan, yakhod Silistre. The first edition was published in 1289 (1872—3).
[2] In the last edition, that of 1308, the authors represented are: Sinán

fully made, partly with the view of showing the development of Ottoman prose, but chiefly in order to supply the young literary aspirant with a series of models which he may study with real advantage. This being the case, the pretentious and wilfully obscure writers of the old time are naturally conspicuous by their absence; there is no word from the Humáyún-Náme or the Shefíq-Náme, while Nergisí and Veysí, those paragons of the Persianists, are mentioned only to be condemned. For not the least valuable and certainly the most interesting feature of the work is a preface and series of critical articles on the authors represented, contributed by the compiler himself. In these, which form the first serious attempt at literary criticism in Turkish, and which are written in a style noteworthy not only for its originality but for its vigour and directness, Tevfíq Bey succeeds in compelling the attention of his readers by the new light in which he presents the literature of his country and by the alternately luminous and suggestive character of his remarks. This work, the preface of which is dated from the Knights' Castle in Rhodes, where the author was imprisoned, was first published in 1296 (1879); it has passed through several editions, each in one way or other an improvement on its predecessor.

In 1299 (1881) Tevfíq Bey, who, along with his colleagues, had been recalled from exile by Murád V during his brief reign, established in Galata a printing-press which very soon gained a high and deserved reputation. The founder, who is a man of cultivated and refined taste, with a keen appreciation of all that is artistic, has from the outset taken the greatest interest in the productions of his establishment,

Pasha, Fuzúlí, Qochi Bey, Na'ímá, Nedím, Kání, Haqqí Pasha, Qoja Segbán-Bashi, Muterjim 'Asim, 'Akif Pasha, Reshíd Pasha, Fu'ád Pasha, Edhem Pertev Pasha, Shinásí, Ziyá Pasha, Sa'd-ulláh Pasha, and Kemál.

sparing neither labour nor expense in his efforts to ensure that these shall be in all ways worthy examples of the typographic art. Nor has his devotion been unrewarded; some of the works issued from this press afford the finest examples in existence of printing in the Oriental characters, surpassing anything hitherto produced either in Europe or in the East.

But beauty of external form has not been the only, or even the chief, concern of Tevfíq Bey; in all his publications he has kept steadily in view that great aim of his party, the education of the people. The Mejmú'a-i Ebu-z-Ziyá, or Ebu-z-Ziyá's Magazine, contains a vast number of useful and instructive articles on an infinity of subjects; the Kutub-Kháne-i Ebu-z-Ziyá, or Ebu-z-Ziyá's Library, is a series of valuable books comprising new editions of rare and interesting old works, reprints of many of the less accessible. writings of the great modern authors, as well as original treatises dealing with matters historical, literary and scientific; while the Lughat-i Ebu-z-Ziyá, or Ebu-z-Ziyá's Dictionary, is in some respects the best Turkish dictionary yet published, and certainly the most interesting, containing, as it does, a wealth of quotations from standard authors of all periods illustrating the various uses of the words explained and the changes in signification which these have undergone. These are but a few of the many works which Ebu-z-Ziyá Tevfíq Bey has printed and published — and often himself written or at least edited — and by means of which he has in his own way done as much as any one man to promote the cause of the new learning.

Ebu-z-Ziyá's, though the most artistic and most interesting, was but one of several printing establishments that were started in the capital about this time. At first the only institution of the kind had been the Imperial Printing-Office;

but later on, when semi-official and private newspapers were
established, each of these had its own press, at which it became
the practice to print books either on account of the proprietor
of the paper, or, as a matter of business, for private persons.
Such books were generally issued at a comparatively low
price, and their cheapness, combined with the facility of
obtaining them, soon began to develop a taste for reading
among the public, so that M. Belin, writing of the position
of letters in Turkey in 1866, speaks of the numerous reading-
rooms and literary societies which were then being established
both in Constantinople and in the provinces. It was not
till some years after this that printing-presses wholly uncon-
nected with any newspaper and destined solely for the
production of books were established. But between 1296 and
1299 (1879—81) a considerable number of such were founded,
one of the earliest and most important being that of the
Armenian Mihrán Efendi, from which many valuable and
creditably executed works have issued. Most of the founders
of these presses are, like Tevfíq Bey and Mihrán Efendi,
publishers as well as printers; but so far there were no
publishers who were not printers.

Thus during these twenty years which we have been
considering the moral and intellectual condition of Turkey
was being profoundly modified; and although the full effects
of the great change then being prepared have not yet
appeared, the signs of it are visible on every hand. A new
conception of Duty has arisen. In old times religion was all
in all. The Turk never thought of himself as a Turk; he
was a Musulmán, and that was enough. The idea of nationality
hardly existed for him. When he went forth to war, it was
not that he might exalt the glory or extend the boundaries
of 'Turkey', for which indeed, strictly speaking, he had not
even a name; when not from mere love of conquest, his

military expeditions were undertaken that infidel or heretic might be brought into obedience to the Servants of God. Of patriotism, as the West understands it, he knew absolutely nothing; he would no more have thought, as some one has said, of dying for his country than of dying for his meridian of longitude.

But now this too is changed, and no word is dearer or more sacred to the modern Turk than that which has been taken to stand for 'Fatherland'. Here again we come upon the hand of Kemál Bey; till his time the word 'watan' had been without associations and comparatively seldom used; but when he raised it from a vague signification hovering between 'home' and 'birthplace' to be the equivalent of the French 'patrie', it became a sacred watchword in the hearts as on the lips of men. Similarly, another word, 'millet', which used to mean a religious community, such as the Roman Catholic or the self-styled 'orthodox' Greek, has been made to do duty as representative of 'the nation' or 'the people' in the modern European acceptations of these terms. That is to say, 'millet' now means either one individual nation among the family of the nations, or the mass of the community in contradistinction to the sovereign and his court, both of which conceptions are new in Turkey. Yet another word which at this time acquired a new and precious significance, and which forms with 'watan and 'millet' the sacred triad of the Ottoman patriot of to-day, is 'ḥurriyyet', that is 'liberty' or 'freedom.'

The Fatherland, the Nation, Liberty, — these three words are the legend on the banner of Young Turkey, and the ideas they represent form the very core of the true and living faith of the regenerated people. This faith, which is now that of practically the whole of the educated portion of the younger generation, and which counts amongst its already mighty army of martyrs some of the very noblest of the race, is the most momentous and in effect far-reaching of the many changes born at this cataclysmic time. Aided by the general spread of education among both sexes and all classes, it has relegated to the background the old dogmatic Muhammedanism, just as in Western Europe the old dogmatic Christianity has been rudely shaken by the popularisation of science and the wide diffusion of all kinds of knowledge. The modern Turkish gentleman still indeed calls himself a Muhammedan, but there is little difference between his attitude towards Islám and that of the typical European scholar of to-day towards Christianity.

In our own immediate subject, a notable, though inevitable result of this has been the deposition of the ʿulemá from their old position of leaders and arbiters of literature. Under the old system, as we have abundantly seen, by virtue of their being generally the most highly educated members of the community, these jurists had always taken a foremost position in every matter connected with learning or culture. But any body at all resembling a priestly caste — though it be as remotely as the ʿulemá — seems by a law of nature ever to be reactionary. So the ʿulemá found no place in their curriculum for the new learning; they could not or would not adapt themselves to the altered condition of affairs, and therefore to-day they are held of no account, while their former place is taken by men of the world, — the diplomatist, the publicist, the journalist.

This period of twenty years is thus the turning-point in the evolution of the new civilisation of Turkey; all that has gone before since the days of the martyred Selím has been leading up to the revolution now accomplished, what follows is its development. In 1859 the Turks were still practically a medieval community; in 1879 they had become a modern nation. Shinásí, Kemál and Ziyá had pointed out the way that they should go; the heroic though unavailing struggle against the hordes of Russia had fanned into white heat the nascent flame of patriotism; the triumph of the constitutional party and the creation of an Ottoman Parliament had come the seeming crown and accomplishment of men's dreams of liberty. For the moment all boded fairer for the moral and intellectual advancement of the Turkish people than ever before in the course of their long history.

CHAPTER II.

SHINÁSÍ EFENDI.

1242—1288 (1826-7—1871).

Ibráhím Shinásí Efendi, the master who laid the foundations of the new learning, was born in the Top-Kháne division of Constantinople in 1242 (1826—7). When little more than a year old he lost his father, a captain in the artillery, who was killed at the defence of Shumla against the Russians in 1828. The child was brought up by some of his mother's relatives, the deceased officer, who was a native of Boli in Asia Minor, having probably no kinsfolk in the capital. After attending the parish school, Shinásí entered the office of the Imperial Arsenal, where he formed a friendship with an elderly and learned clerk named Ibráhím Efendi, with whose assistance he acquired the Arabic and Persian tongues, and at whose suggestion he committed to memory more than half of the huge Arabic dictionary called the Qámús. Amongst the European officers at this time employed in the Arsenal was a certain Châteauneuf, who afterwards adopted Islám and became known as Reshád Bey. From him Shinásí received some lessons in the French language, which created in him a great desire to become more intimately acquainted with the culture and civilisation of the West. His opportunity was not long in coming, for shortly afterwards he heard that the authorities were looking for a young man of his own age — some seventeen years — who might proceed to Europe for the purpose of studying certain branches of western science. Shinásí's difficulty was how to bring himself under notice, for, being of a shy and retiring disposition, he had always avoided paying court to the great, and consequently was without a patron to push his interests. His friend Reshád Bey came to his assistance, and advised him to apply directly to Fethí Pasha the governor of the arsenal, suggesting to him at the same time how and when he should do this.

So in conformity with Reshád's plan, one day when Sultan ʿAbd-ul-Mejíd was visiting the Arsenal, and Fethí Pasha was standing in the exercising-ground in full view of the Imperial Kiosque, Shinásí stepped forward, and, having saluted the governor in military fashion, represented how he had studied hard, and, besides acquiring Arabic and Persian, had learned a little French, and how it would be a good and advantageous thing to select him to be sent to Europe. The naïveté of the young man's speech pleased the Pasha, who promised to find an opportunity to lay his case before the Sultan. So when shortly afterwards Fethí Pasha was summoned into the Imperial presence, ʿAbd-ul-Mejíd, who had seen a young man in the dress of a clerk come out into the exercise-ground and exchange some words with the governor, asked the Pasha who his interlocutor was and what he desired. The Pasha accordingly represented to His Majesty the young clerk's request; and that same day Shinásí was received in audience by the amiable ʿAbd-ul-Mejíd, who spoke to him in kindly and encouraging terms. A week later Shinásí was sent to Paris with a monthly allowance of 750 francs, and the future of Ottoman literature was determined.

In the French capital the young Turk made the acquaintance of the family of the great orientalist De Sacy, who some dozen years before had himself befriended Reshíd Bey, the illustrious Reshíd Pasha of later days, on his arrival as a stranger in the western world. Introductions soon followed to many of the leading men of letters in Paris, including Ernest Renan and the poet Lamartine; and in their society Shinásí found ample means to gratify his taste for European culture, while at the same time he assimilated the principles which were to guide him in the great work of his life. For although Shinásí did not neglect the ostensible object of his sojourn in France, and we read of his studying the economic and even the physical sciences, it was to literature and things literary that the best, because the sincerest, efforts of his mind were directed.

On his return to Constantinople [1] Shinásí was offered by Reshíd Pasha, then Grand Vezir, employment in both the Ministry of Public Instruction and the Treasury, but he contented himself with a post in the first only of these departments. He was also made a member of the Enjumen-i Dánish, the Imperial Academy of Science and Literature, which had just been established under the auspices of Sultan ʿAbd-ul-Mejíd. But, being a protégé of Reshíd Pasha, Shinásí incurred the ill-will of that statesman's rivals, Fuʾád and ʿAlí Pashas, who took advantage of Reshíd's deposition from the Grand Vezirate to accomplish his client's dismissal from

[1] The biographers do not mention the dates of Shinásí's departure from and return to Constantinople, neither do they tell us how long he stayed in France. We know that he was there as late as 1266 (1849—50), for some of his letters from Paris bearing that date have been published; and as he was on his return made a member of the Enjumen-i Dánish (opened in the Shevwál of 1267 (August 1851) which is spoken of as having been then newly formed, it is probable that he returned about the end of 1851 or beginning of 1852.

his office in the Ministry of Public Instruction as well as his expulsion from the Imperial Academy and his exclusion from a financial appointment given to him by the ex-Prime Minister, bringing forward as justification for this persecution some ridiculous charge as to their victim having shaved his beard while in Paris.[1] Upon this Shinásí addressed a qasída to Reshíd Pasha in which he reflected upon the conduct of Fu'ád and ʿAlí and also upon the behaviour of ʿArif Hikmet, the poet Sheykhu'l-Islám who was president of the Imperial Academy. The persons thus attacked were about to meet this move by impeaching the poet, when Reshíd's return to power set matters right, and re-instated Shinásí in his former position. On the death of Reshíd Pasha in 1274 (1858), Yúsuf Kámil Pasha, who afterwards translated Fénelon's Télémaque, became Shinásí's protector; but out of respect for the deceased statesman who had done so much for Turkey, Fu'ád and ʿAlí refrained from taking any steps against his client.

Official duties were, however, but little to Shinásí's taste, and moreover he perceived that so long as he was connected either with the government service or with state institutions he would be hampered and impeded in what he felt to be the true work of his life. He therefore resigned both his official position and his membership of the Imperial Academy that he might henceforth be free to devote himself entirely to his arduous work, a step he would probably have taken earlier but for deference to his patron Reshíd Pasha.

In 1276 (1859—60) Shinásí took the first public step towards the accomplishment of his aim by starting, in con-

---

[1] There used to be a prejudice amongst the Turks against a man who shaved his beard after having once allowed it to grow. Fu'ád and ʿAlí Pashas were both men of much talent and ability, and far too enlightened to be influenced by any such childish notions; they merely exploited a vulgar prejudice in order to compass their own ends.

junction with a friend named Ágáh Efendi, a newspaper which he called Terjumán-i Aḥwál or 'The Interpreter of Events'. After six months he withdrew from this paper, and in the year 1278 (1861—2), he began to publish his far more famous journal, the Tasvír-i Efkár or 'Tablet of Opinions'.

Towards the end of the following year, 1279 (1863), he was joined by Námiq Kemál Bey, whose youthful allegiance he at once and for ever secured, and whom he trained to be not only the doughtiest champion of the new learning, but the greatest master of Turkish prose who has ever taken pen in hand.

The publication of this second newspaper marks an epoch in the history both of Ottoman literature and of the Ottoman language. Not merely was it the first unofficial journal in Turkey; it is the first utterance of the Modern School, that School which was destined in the brief space of twenty years to sweep from the stage the crumbling débris of five centuries of Asiaticism. Here for the first time an Ottóman man of letters, conversant with and appreciative of a great European language and literature, deliberately sets to work to reconstruct from its very foundations the whole edifice of Turkish literary style. How he went to work upon this noble but stupendous task, and with what measure of success his efforts were attended, we shall ere long see.

Even those who opposed Shinásí's principles were compelled to admit his courage and ability; and it is pleasant to know that Fu'ád Pasha, who was at heart a friend to progress, lived not only to regret the part he had formerly played, but to receive Shinásí into his circle, and solicit and obtain his co-operation in establishing the 'Military Gazette'. [1] Thanks to the esteem of Fu'ád Pasha and the patronage

---

[1] Jeríde-i ᶜAskeriyye.

of Yúsuf Kámil, the ill-will of ʿAlí Pasha was overcome; and it was determined to make Shinásí a member of the Supreme Court, and at the same time to promote him to the First Grade. But Shinásí loved freedom and hated office, and so, to escape having to accept an honour which he could not well refuse, he quietly slipped off to Paris, leaving the young Kemál Bey in charge of his journal.

This occurred in 1281 (1864—5), and during the next few years Shinásí remained in the French capital busying himself with the compilation of a huge lexicon of the Turkish language, in preparing and arranging the materials for which he examined nearly all the Oriental books likely to be of service that are preserved in the Bibliothèque Nationale. This gigantic work was however, never completed; Shinásí was compelled to stop half way, at the letter ط. Of the fourteen great volumes, each comprising a thousand pages, in which the author's manuscript is contained, some are in the possession of the French Asiatic Society, of which Shinásí was a member, while some found their way into the library of the Hungarian collector Dániel Szilágyi, and are now preserved in the university of Buda-Pesth.

When Sultan ʿAbd-ul-ʿAzíz visited Paris in the summer of 1867, Fu'ád Pasha, who was in the Imperial suite, had a private interview with Shinásí in that city during which he entreated him to return to Turkey and assume the governorship of the province of Smyrna. Fu'ád's persuasions were apparently successful; but soon after Shinásí's arrival in Constantinople he induced the Pasha to allow him to return to Paris to collect some documents he had left behind and to arrange certain private affairs. While he · was absent, Fu'ád died at Nice (Shevwál 1285 = February 1869); so Shinásí remained in the French capital till the outbreak of the Franco-German war in July 1870, when he again returned to Constantinople. There he died on the 5th of Rejeb 1288 (13th September 1871) of inflammation of the brain, brought on, it is said, by the arduous nature of the work on which he had been so long engaged. His death occurred exactly a week after that of ʿAlí Pasha.

Shinásí was, we are told, of a quiet and meditative disposition, speaking but little and in short sentences. When he did speak, his language was terse and concise, and his words were straight to the point. He was very patient and gentle when talking with ignorant or prejudiced people, but used to be displeased if during a serious conversation anyone tried to turn the subject into jest, a proceeding which he looked upon as equivalent to a confession of defeat.

Shinásí is justly regarded as the true founder of the Modern School of Ottoman literature, since he was the first who seriously and systematically strove to raise that literature from being as hitherto a mere plaything for the amusement of the learned into an instrument for the moral and intellectual education of the whole people. The way in which this change might be most surely and most readily effected was the great lesson which Shinásí learned from the West. That way was, briefly, the substitution of the natural for the artificial, involving the subordination of manner to matter, and the adjustment of style to subject. But to accomplish this end it was necessary profoundly to modify the existing Turkish literary idiom. Shinásí felt this, and himself indicated the lines along which such a modification should be made. Other writers before him had indeed endeavoured, though hardly with his object, to refashion the literary idiom, and had at times even met with a partial success. But their success had never been more than partial, and never very far-reaching in result. This was because their efforts had necessarily been only tentative; those would-be reformers

had known of no guide whom they could unhesitatingly
follow; all their light had come from within; and it is
doubtful whether any one among them had ever quite realised
either what his ultimate object was, or in what manner it
was to be attained.

Where Shinásí differed from all his predecessors was that
he knew exactly what he wanted to do, and how to accomplish
it. In the literature of France he had a model which displayed
to perfection all that he desired. He found there an idiom
at once concise, clear and elegant, admirably adapted to
convey with happily-mingled simplicity and grace those moral
and intellectual lessons which he held to be the true end
of literature.

His work then lay plain before him; it was to create in
Turkish a corresponding literary idiom. This Shinásí began
to do; and his successors have most ably carried on the
work. But the method they have followed is very unlike
that adopted by the early Turkish scholars who, when they
thought to Persianise their language, annexed the whole of
the Persian dictionary and practically the whole of the
Persian grammar. Shinásí and his followers have not sought
to introduce French words and French grammatical rules
into Turkish (though some such have almost accidentally
crept in); they have looked rather to see how ideas are
expressed in French and what standards of literary taste
there prevail, and have striven in the light of the lessons
thus learned to make their language at once simpler and
stronger, and to fit it to hold a place among the languages
of modern Europe.

The great principle underlying this revolution is, as I
have said, the predominance of the natural over the artificial.
Shinásí at once perceived that this entailed the development
of the hitherto neglected Turkish core of the language, the

first step towards which was the clearing away of the huge
mass of useless accretions and false embellishments under
which so many centuries of Persianism had well nigh smothered
whatever was vital in the written speech. And such was
the hearty good-will wherewith the reformer set about this
work of stripping off the tattered tinsel of the past, that
Tevfíq Bey has somewhere described him as the Death-Angel
(ʿAzrá'íl) of literary solecisms. The development of the
Turkish core of the language, then, has all along been one
of the objects of the Modern School; but this has been
sought by natural, not by artificial means. There has been
no attempt to replace long-established and thoroughly naturalised Persian or Arabic words by half-forgotten Tartar
wraiths; a mirror is still called áyna, not gözgü; Paradise
is still named jennet, not uchmaq. What has been done is
to study and systematise the heretofore absolutely neglected
Turkish grammar, to discover and then turn to account the
resources latent in the native idiom, and to give literary
form to many a forceful and idiomatic turn of speech hitherto
confined exclusively to the vernacular. [1]

In attempting thus to revolutionise the literature of his
country, Shinásí was to outward appearances running counter
to the spirit of his time, but in reality he was acting in
harmony with its deeper tendencies. Apparently he was
running counter to the spirit of his age, for we have seen
that at this time a Persianist revival held the field, and
any recrudescence of Persianism necessarily implied the
strengthening of the artificial. But that his labours were in
truth in harmony with deeper-seated and more lasting tendencies, though as yet these were working beneath the
surface silently and in secret, is proved by the completeness

[1] One of Shinásí's minor innovations was the introduction of punctuation
into Turkish writing and printing.

of the revolution whereby within a decade of his death the whole current literature of Turkey — prose and poetry alike — was transformed and remodelled upon the very lines that he laid down.

When we reflect upon the magnitude of Shinásí's services, how he led Turkish literature back to healthy and vigorous life from the very gates of death, pointing to the great masters, Truth and Nature, and showing where the lessons taught by these were to be most fully and freely learned, and how he ennobled for his countrymen the aim and purpose of literature, we can well understand the intense admiration with which he is regarded by his disciples, and are ready to excuse those loyal followers if at times in the enthusiasm of their gratitude they attribute to their beloved and revered master more than the critic further distant and less beholden may find it easy to allow.

It in no wise detracts from the very high credit which is most justly Shinásí's due, neither is it the slightest disparagement to the unquestionably great value of his work, to say that had that illustrious reformer never arisen, the revolution which he inaugurated would none the less have come about, and that almost at the moment when it did. The reforms of Sultan Mahmúd's reign had familiarised men with the idea of change, and when the study of the French language and literature became fairly general among the educated classes, it was inevitable that ere long some man should arise possessed of sufficient insight to see that salvation for Turkish literature, as for all things Turkish, was to be found in the assimilation, so far as that was practicable, of the spirit of the West, and endowed with sufficient energy and courage to carry his convictions into practice. If any proof were required of this assertion, it would be enough to point to Ziyá Pasha who was at this very time independently developing a literary idiom from the same models as Shinásí, and with hardly less success.

Again, it is rather through his example and precept than through anything he actually achieved that the influence of Shinásí has been effective; and here his position is curiously analogous to that of his predecessor Ahmed Pasha, who brought about the Classic movement by drawing attention to the methods of Newá'í and his circle, not by the excellence of the work he himself produced.

Leaving out of sight the uncompleted Lexicon which, never having been published, can have had no effect, the amount of Shinásí's written work is comparatively small. All his most serious efforts, moreover, are in prose, and consist almost entirely of articles political, literary, and social, which he wrote for different newspapers, notably for his own journal the Tasvír-i Efkár.

The intensely practical turn of his mind and the strong feeling that he had for precision were unfavourable to the cultivation of poetry. Verse was with him merely a relaxation. His own best efforts and those of his immediate followers were directed to the creation of a prose style; poetry was not looked upon by them as a very serious matter, and for the time being was left to shift for itself.

It is therefore not surprising that Shinásí's work in verse is limited in extent and for the most part playful in tone. He has, however, a few religious· pieces, especially one hymn, characterised by considerable power and dignity. But his most remarkable work is the series of translations which he made from the French. With the exception of one of La Fontaine's Fables, The Wolf and the Lamb, which is rendered in its entirety, the passages translated are mere fragments, chiefly from Racine and Lamartine. No attempt is made to preserve either the metre or the form of the originals, but the meaning is presented with accuracy and vigour.

It is the appearance of the little volume containing these translations, which was first issued in a lithographed edition in 1859,[1] that I take as the starting-point of the Modern School of Ottoman poetry. It is true that this little book had practically no immediate effect, and it is true that the real modern poetry of Turkey was not developed until twenty years later, but none the less these translations of Shinásí mark the turning-point in the history of Ottoman poetry. For in them breathes for the first time that spirit which is to vitalise and inspire the future. They are the earliest verses in the Turkish language to exhibit any indication that such a thing as European poetry is known to exist. All the Ottoman poetry of the past has been developed in complete ignorance of Western culture, and it would not have differed in one single whit had no line of French verse ever been penned. The Ottoman poetry of the future owes well-nigh all that it has and is — form and substance, inspiration and imagery — to the example of France. Surely this little book of Shinásí, which brings for the first time into Ottoman poetry an echo of that magic song which is to work so mighty a transformation, must be conceded an importance far beyond anything to which by its intrinsic merits it might lay claim. It stands here a landmark on the frontier between Asia and Europe, it shines out a beacon-fire signalling the passing of the old order and the advent of the new.

His study of La Fontaine inspired Shinásí to write versified fables on his own account. Three such occur in the printed editions of his poems, and are named respectively 'The Ass

[1] A second (printed) edition was issued from the office of the Tasvír-i Efkár in Ramazán 1287 (end of 1870).

and the Fox', 'The Young Eagle and the Crow', and 'The Mosquito and the Bee'. These, especially the first two, are written in very homely, even colloquial language; there is nothing quite like them before in Turkish poetry.

Something of their manner is to be observed in several among a group of little pieces which we may describe as occasional verses. These deal with very various matters, and are often very short, sometimes consisting of a single couplet. The language is generally quite simple, and in a few instances the poet has amused himself by using only pure Turkish words, avoiding everything borrowed from Arabic or Persian. A similar effect would be obtained in English by the exclusive employment of words of Teutonic origin and the rejection of all derived from French, Latin or Greek. In neither case could the result be anything beyond a tour de force. It should, however, be said that in the selection of his Turkish words Shinásí has shown good taste, and so his verses are not marred by the uncouthness which disfigures those of certain of the Romanticist poets. These occasional verses are, along with the Fables, the most characteristic of their author's metrical works; they are pervaded by a genial and playful spirit, but of true poetic feeling there are few traces.

For the rest, Shinásí's little Díwán contains a few qasídas and ghazels and a fair number of chronograms. These are all in the old style, of which they are poor examples, possessing neither interest nor merit. The ghazels especially are particularly frigid and lifeless; so earnest an advocate of literary sincerity was hardly likely to be at his best where conventionality was the standard of success.

Shinásí's series of translations from the French is by a long way his most important work so far as the history of Ottoman poetry is concerned; but an English translation of Turkish verses which are themselves translations from the

French would obviously illustrate nothing. Instead therefore of offering such, I shall give further on a selection
of the French verses translated by Shinásí, the Turkish
renderings of which will be found in their place among the
texts in another volume.

This is the Hymn which I have mentioned as being
probably the finest of Shinásí's poetical works.

Hymn [459].

God the Highest, He the Monarch of the world of majesty,
Omnipresent is; no throne-room in His palace may there be.
The vast Kingdom of Eternity is His, and His alone;
Numberless the everlasting stars that always there have shone.
Lo, the edifice of Earth and Heaven stands, His wisdom's sign;
Void and peopled, all existent, is His hand of power's design.
All the angels laud His splendour and His majesty and might,
Low the Sphere in adoration bows before His glory bright.
As He biddeth, ever onward day and night careers the earth,
Seasons change, and bounteous springtide blooms again in freshened birth.
Sun and moon are sparks of radiance from His mercy's fostering beam,
From His anger — if from aught — is litten the infernal leam.
Yon effulgent stars are flashes of His majesty most high,
'Tis their lustrous sheen that gildeth all the cupole of the sky;
Fixed are some and others wandering by the Omnipotent decree;
Each one is a shining proof that God in very truth doth be.
Though to prove His being where the need of this terrestrial ball,
When one mote by Him created were enough, enough for all?
All too weak to see His Essence is His creatures' earthly sight,
Yet the vision of the understanding may perceive His Light.
To my intellect 'tis needful to confess His Unity,
To my heart and soul 'tis needful to adore His Majesty.
Fain am I before His Signs in ecstasy to bow me low,
Learn ye thence what else I fain would for my loved Creator do.
O Shinásí, deep the fear of God is burned into my soul;
Though my lips may smile, the tears of blood forth from my heart's eye roll.
Penitence for my transgression doth my spirit overbear;

What can I? — I dare no prayer for pardon with this fell despair!
What said I? — Oh! I repent me! that too was a deed of guile,
This excuse that I have proffered than my sin is yet more vile!
How should not the Light of Mercy bid my sad face smile again?
Which is greater, God's Compassion or my foul rebellion's stain?
Does not then His boundless Graciousness the whole wide world embrace?
Else does this poor slave, though in the world, find in the world no place?
Though His servant's faults, for all his frailty, great and grievous bé,
Does not His compassion o'er His anger gain the victory?
From His servant's native frailty 'tis his errors still proceed,
In the World Unseen He therefore for His folk doth intercede.
Grace of God, divine and free, to pardon me will well avail;
Deem not, God forefend! that Mercy limitless shall ever fail.

The Ass and the Fox is the most interesting of the poet's original Fables.

The Ass and the Fox [460].

From a vineyard once an aged ass was slowly toiling down
With a load of 'beauty's faces'[1] he was bearing to the town.
Lo behold, just then a hungry fox before his eyes appeared, —
Eager longing for the luscious grapes had all his vitals seared.
Kicked a bit at first the donkey when the other came him nigh,
But his waywardness and coyness were not long in passing by.

The Fox: —

'O my lion, brave and mighty, may not I approach to thee,
'So that I may see thee near? Thy loveliness dumbfounders me!
'May the shadow of the favour of my lord abide for aye!
'Wheresoe'er yon blessed feet have trodden, blossom roses gay.
'Yonder tail so sweetly scented all would rarest musk suppose;
'Fain I'd smell it, if my master would not kick me on the nose.
'In those speaking eyes thine inward virtues and thy culture shine;
'Words poetic and melodious well beseem that mouth of thine!'

[1] Rú-yi Nigár, 'beauty's face', is the name of a variety of grape of a light pink colour.

Hereupon the donkey mightily delighted brayed a deal
Just as though he'd seen a tender thistle or a melon-peel. [1]

The Fox : —

'Ah, that charming voice hath reached e'en to the very heart of me;
'While if thou art silent, lo, another lovesome joy have we;
'For the nightingale hath heard thee, and to steal thy notes is fain,
'Singing so that to the listener comes a gentle sense of pain.'

Thus the fox went on a-prattling, laughing slyly at his fere,
Till that he had brought the donkey where a well was deep and clear.

The Fox : —

'Down there is a lovely stable where are feeds in goodly store;
'But alack! one cannot enter laden, narrow is the door.
'Pleasures many such as sleeping and as resting still are there;
'Eating feeds and drinking water are the only toil and care.
'Then the lady donkeys dwelling there have quite a special grace;
'Just look in, but see thou be not smitten by some pretty face.'

Then the ass went near and gazed down on the liquid mirror bright,
Saw his face therein reflected, — watered then his mouth forthright.

The Ass : —

'Yes indeed, a face all lovely and all gracious there I see.'

The Fox : —

'Call her then to come beside thee that thy playmate she may be.'

All excited, loudly bellowed out the donkey's 'Come thou here!'
From the well his words re-echoed fell upon his wildered ear.

The Fox : —

'Hear'st thou not how to that noble banquet they are calling thee?
'Sore I wonder is there ne'er a place as servant there for me?

---

[1] In Turkey donkeys are often given melon-peel, of which they are very fond. قابوق كورمش اشك كبى, 'Like an ass that has seen a melon-skin', is popularly said of one who is taken up with a trifle, the figure being derived from the donkey's habit of making for any piece of peel which he may see on the roadside and from which it is difficult to get him away.

'Leave thy burden here, and free from all impediments descend,
'I shall follow straight behind thee there as lackey to attend.'

Then the donkey cast his load to earth, himself into the well,
Thus unto the fox to heir him and to pray for him [1] it fell.

All the following are examples of what I have called
Shináeí's occasional verses. The special names which some
of them bear is a new feature in Turkish poetry; it is of
course adopted from the French. The love-poem which follows is mere badinage; but it is quite original both in
language and expression, and contains a number of fancies
and similes that are absolutely new.

Declaration of Love [461].

My heart hath chosen for its love a matchless beauty bright,
And jealous is it grown, alack, e'en of my very sight.
How passing well do yonder breasts beseem her bosom fair,
As 'twere two guelder-roses that a tender branchlet bare.
Though yonder bosom into mine at times is ardent prest,
Think not thereby the pang of love is driven from my breast.
More dainty than the jessamine yon shapely figure slight;
If ivy-like I clasp it, it will bend to me forthright.
Since I have held heart-converse with that charmer young and free,
I seek none other, houri fair or angel though she be.
When overcome of fond desire, those eyes, a-fainting, swoon,
They waken when my tears are o'er her lovesome face bestrewn.
Shall not the heart within me melt when smile those languid eyes?
The sweet words from her lips that flow bid all my yearning rise.
A-blush at her own beauty, lo, her cheeks with crimson glow;
To veil that bashful face of hers the tresses o'er it flow.
I'm fallen sick of yearning ever dreaming of her hair;
Was 't thus, I wonder, Mejnún did for Leylá frenzied fare?

[1] To pray for the repose of his soul. Certain passages from the Koran,
notably the 36th chapter, that entitled Yá Sín, are frequently read or recited
for the repose of the souls of the dead.

I'll give my life to her and toss no more in mortal pain; [1]
What right has he who loves a dear to spend his life in vain?
I'd dig my grave before I die, the martyr of her love,
And with my tears of blood I'd write upon the stone thereof.

During his conversations with the European savants Shinásí
doubtless heard something about the speculations of Darwin;
probably he never really understood the theory of the great
naturalist; at any rate the doctrine of the mutability of
species seems to have been little to his liking.

A Tale of Transmigration [462].

A sham philosopher of scant esteem
Was wont himself Pythagoras to deem.
The transmigration of the soul his creed,
Disintegration of the frame his rede.
He said: 'The beast that sticketh up his tail [2]
'Will come in human form withouten fail.'
A wise man heard the words that ox [3] did say,
And with this answer stopped his mouth with hay: [4]
'How can I question this religion's truth
'With thee thyself alive to prove its sooth?'

To an Artist's Wife [463].

'Tis meet that on my heart the image of thy form I trace,
E'en as the artist on his canvass limns an angel's face.
   I marvel, is it thy fair face, or is it thy sweet soul,
That to his heart who looks on thee reveals Celestial grace?

[1] A reminiscence of the proverb جـان چـكشمـهدنـسـه اولك يـكـدر
'Tis better to die than to be in the throes of death.'
[2] To stick up or erect the tail (as dogs do when they approach each
other) is familiarly said of a man who assumes an aggressively haughty air.
Shinásí would here show his contempt for what he conceived to be the
insolence and presumption of those whose views he is ridiculing.
[3] A stupid fool is sometimes called an 'ox' in Turkish, as he is an 'ass'
or a 'goose'.
[4] 'Shut him up'.

The following four lines are amongst those in which Turkish words alone are employed; I have imitated the original by using only Teutonic words in the translation.

Verse [464].

Who sees the gleaming of thy brow amid thy dusky locks
Would deem that midst of darkling clouds the sun is risen fair.
Would not he say who sees me by thy side in tears of blood,
'Lo, yonder, one whom the sea-maid [1] hath drowned a-lying there.'

This 'quatrain of condolence', sent to a bereaved friend, is one of the prettiest things that Shinásí wrote.

Quatrain [465].

May the God of might and glory deck the Heavenly garden-close
With the fruitage of thy heart that Death now in the dust bestows!
Ah! how Death is like the bitter blast that all untimely blows,
Tearing from the branch the blossom which amid the mire it throws.

Here are two independent couplets.

Couplet [466].

My being doth to my Creator's being witness bear;
Superfluous were other proofs, however strong they were.

Couplet written in Paris [467].

Though I am far from my dear home, why should I feel distrest? —
Thus runs the proverb: God doth build the stranger bird a nest. [2]

[1] Su qizi 'the sea-maid', or more commonly, su malikesi 'the sea-queen', is the mermaid or siren. The Turks derived their notions of such a being from their Greek neighbours. The Persians know nothing of her, so she does not figure in their literature, and consequently not in that of the old Ottomans; but the men of the Modern School, carrying out and extending a practice begun by the Romanticists, adopt into their verses beautiful fancies or legends wheresoever they find them, so the 'sea-queen' is pretty often to be met with in the newer poetry.

[2] غريب قوشكڭ يوواسنى اللّٰه ياپـار 'God builds the stranger bird's nest,' a well-known proverb meaning that God is the helper of the helpless.

CHAPTER III.

ZIYÁ PASHA.

1245—1297 (1829-30—1880).

If we were studying the history of Ottoman literature, and not merely that of Ottoman poetry, this chapter would be devoted to the life and work of Kemál Bey. That author was, as we have seen, trained directly by Shinásí Efendi, of whose principles and aims he became the immediate heir. As he thus directly carried on the work of the master, this would be the natural place in which to consider his career and labours; but seeing that his best and most characteristic poetry is all in the modern style, I have thought it advisable to defer doing so until we have learned something of the nature of this new style and of the manner of its introduction. We shall thereupon pass on to Ziyá Pasha, the third of the illustrious triumvirate.

ᶜAbd-ul-Hamíd Ziyá, that Ziyá Pasha whose criticisms on the earlier poets we have so often quoted, was universally known as Ziyá Bey until a very few years before his death when he received the rank of vezír, which bears with it the title of pasha. He was born in Constantinople in 1245

4

(1829—30),[1] just three years after Shinásí. Some forty years afterwards when he had mastered French and created for himself a charmingly simple and lucid style, Ziyá Bey made a translation of Jean Jacques Rousseau's 'Emil'. To this he prefixed a preface of his own, dealing with the education question in Turkey, in the course of which he gives a most interesting account of his own childhood. This I shall translate in its entirety, not only for the sake of the biographical details it contains and the glimpses of Turkish child-life it affords, but because it will serve to show something of the marvellous change which even then had been effected in the character of Ottoman prose.[2]

'My father', begins Ziyá, 'who was a clerk in the Galata custom-house, was a thrifty man who understood his business and was content with his salary. During my childhood we lived summer and winter alike[3] at Qandilli on the Bosphorus. My father bought a Circassian slave-boy, called 'Omer, who was some seventeen or eighteen years of age, to accompany me to school and to do the household errands. As this slave had in his own country been brought up to thieving, he

---

[1] This is the date given by Fatín Efendi. Tevfíq Bey gives 1241 (1825—6). Both authorities knew Ziyá personally; but in this case I prefer the former, as the date he gives tallies better with Ziyá's statement in the preface to the Kharábát that at the time he was writing he had passed his forty-fourth year. This would give 1289 (1872—3) as the date of the preface; the Kharábát was published in 1291 (1874—5). Had Ziyá been born in 1241, his forty-fourth year would have fallen in 1285; but we know that from 1284 to 1288 he was in voluntary exile in Europe, while the Kharábát was not compiled till after his return to Turkey.

[2] This preface was published in the second volume of Ebu-z-Ziyá's Magazine (Mejmú'a-i Ebú-z-Ziyá) under the title of 'Ziyá Pasha's Story of his Childhood' ضيا پاشانڭ اوان طفوليتى حقّنده‌كى مـقـالهسى. The portion translated occurs in Nos. 14 and 15, issued respectively on the 1st. and 15th of the Latter Rebí' 1298 (March, 1881).

[3] Not removing into Constantinople for the winter, as is usual.

used when the cherries and grapes were ripe, to take me along with him to the vineyards and steal such fruit as he could reach, which we would eat together. One day, when I must have been six or seven years old, we went together to a vineyard called the Tank Vineyard (Hawuzlu Bágh), which was one of those above Qandilli belonging to the ex-Grand Admiral Dámád Khalíl Pasha. As this vineyard was protected by thorny shrubs which surrounded it on every side, the slave could find no way to get in. So he parted the shrubs with a stick that he had, and made a little hole. "I can't squeeze through there", said he to me, "but you are little; in you go, pull the grapes from the vines near you, hand them out to me, and we'll eat them together." "All right", said I, and pushing my way in, I set to work to gather the grapes.

'Now it happened that just then Khalíl Pasha had come into that particular vineyard to practise shooting, and as it so chanced that the jug for the mark[1] had been set up at the very spot where I was making my raid, he saw me in the distance. Now there was in his household a qawas[2] called Qandillili Ahmed Bey[3] who had tremendous moustachios which used to frighten me whenever I met him. On that day he was in attendance on the Pasha, who pointed me out to him and told him to bring me before him. As for me, I was quite unconscious of the presence of anyone and was busy pulling grapes and handing them through the hedge to the slave, when all of a sudden some one came

---

[1] An ordinary earthenware jug is a very common target for practice with the musket. Many of the earlier poets have chronograms on the 'breaking of the jug' by some royal or distinguished marksman.

[2] A qawas (originally qawwás 'a bowman') was formerly a man-at-arms attached to a great man's household; nowadays the name is given to certain armed servants attached to the public offices and foreign embassies.

[3] That is, Ahmed Bey of Qandilli.

up from behind and caught me in his arms. Far from seeking
to frighten me, he managed to reassure and quiet me, and
so brought me up to the Pasha who pushed in front of me
a plate of grapes that was lying before him, and invited
me to eat some. This kindly act of his quite removed my
fear and shyness, and I began to eat without more ado. He
then asked me whose child I was and where our house was
situated, and I told him. Then he asked how I came to
be stealing grapes, whereupon, concealing nothing, I told
him all that the slave had taught me to do. My candour
and truthfulness were quite apparent and they pleased the
Pasha, so he put some money into my hand and sent me
home in charge of Ahmed Bey. [1]

'Some time after this, my father freed the slave and sent
him back to his own country; while I was sent to the
School of Humanities, [2] which had recently been opened

[1] Ziyá Pasha has here the following note: — 'During the late Khalíl
Pasha's last Grand-Admiralship I was, as Fate determined, in the personal
service of the Sultan. One day the Pasha came to the Imperial palace, and
while I was conversing with him the incident mentioned above came into my
mind, and I said, 'Do you remember how, some sixteen or seventeen years
ago, when you were practising in the Tank Vineyard at Qandilli, you once
saw a child in a green gown stealing grapes, and sent the qawas Ahmed
Bey to fetch him, and how you treated him with great kindness?' The Pasha,
who was very intelligent and sharp-witted, at once remembered and said, 'To
this day I am sorry for that child, for his father, whoever he was, had
entrusted him to a thief of a slave; but as for the child himself, I could
see no signs of anything bad in him, for he told me all about the matter,
hiding nothing, and he pleased me much. Ahmed Bey, too, afterwards cor-
roborated what the child had said. But how come you to know anything
about that child or that affair?' I answered, 'That child whom you treated
with such undeserved kindness when you caught him stealing grapes in your
vineyard is now a bearded man, and it is he who has the honour of addressing
you.' No sooner had I said this than the Pasha blushed, so great was his
modesty, as though it were he who had been the thief, and not permitting
me to thank him, he overwhelmed me with his graciousness.'

[2] The School of Humanities — Mekteb-i Edebiyye — was in its day a
well-known educational institution; it is no longer in existence.

near the Suleymániyya Mosque, under the direction of the late Imám-záde; and a lala,[1] whose name was Isma'íl Agha and whose age was from fifty-five to sixty years, was engaged to superintend my education.

'My lala, who was a native of a village in the district of Qaysariyya,[2] had served as page to certain vezírs in the provinces at the time of the janissaries, and had seen many things and knew the world fairly well; he was in truth a competent and experienced man. He was most anxious to be reunited to his children; indeed his thought and care day and night was how to gain a few piastres so that he might some day return to his own country and pass his closing years amongst his family. So when it came to the question of money the lala would forget all his duties as a man. Thus although my father's first injunction both to the lala and myself was that I should not go into the mosque courtyard and play with the little ragamuffins, we used every day when I came out of school to go for a turn with my companions in the courtyard of the Suleymániyya Mosque. If the lala looked as though he might prove a little fractious, I would take from my pocket twenty or thirty ˉparas, what remained of the daily allowance given me by my father, and slip them into his hand, whereon he would smile and say, "Oh dear! I have not said the afternoon prayer, go and play while I say it." And after the prayer he would most often fall asleep amongst the worshippers outside the mosque, and leave me to myself for an hour or two. Afterwards we would together arrange some story to tell my father, should he on our return ask why we were late.

---

[1] There is no English equivalent to the Turkish lala, who is a male slave or man-servant to whom the care of a child is given, in short a kind of male nursery-governess.

[2] In the original the name of the village is given as اڤكك.

'But for all this my lala was never remiss in encouraging me in every way he could to apply myself to my studies and to strive to surpass the other children in my class. Indeed my beginning to write poetry was owing to the influence of this man, and as it was brought about in a curious way, it may not be without interest to relate it here.

·My lala was very fond of poetry; for all that his spelling was so bad that it .was difficult to read what he wrote, he was for ever, in season and out of season, reciting verses which he knew by heart from ꜥAshiq ꜥOmer and Gevherí. [1] At times too he would compose things something like qitꜥas or ghazels, which occasionally contained lines in metre. This is the opening couplet of a ghazel of his:

"The anguish of my heart do I with pen unto this page declare;
"Let's see what thing will hap, what it will say unto the rose-lipped fair." [2]

'A teacher of Persian named ꜥÍsá Efendi had been appointed to my school, and came on the Tuesday of each week. Some of the children took lessons from him; but as this counsel which my father gave me when I was sent to the school, "Take good heed that you do not learn Persian, for 'who Persian read lose half their creed,'" [3] hung like an earring in my ear, I, far from having any hankerings after Persian, looked upon those who learned it as infidels.

'My lala, who was aware of this, explained to me privately how Persian was necessary for everything; how it was possible to learn it without hurt to one's religion; how every

---

[1] [ꜥAshiq (Lover) is the title given to a class of wandering half erotic, half mystic poets to which the two troubadours here named belonged. E. G. B.]

[2] درونم دردین عــرض ایتدم بــو قرطاسه قلملرئـه
کورهم نـه ظهور ایلر نـه سویلر غنـچه فلرلـه

[3] هر کیم اوقور فارسی گیدر دینک یاریسی. This well-known jingle expresses the wide-spread prejudice against Persian which used to exist among ignorant Turks, who looked upon it as the special language of heresy and of the mysticism which to them was atheism.

one who read Persian was not an infidel, ʿÍsá Efendi, for instance, being a very pious and religious man; how he himself regretted that he had not learned it long ago, and would, if that were possible, learn it even now when his beard was white; how if I did not learn it I should be beaten by my companions when the examination-time came; how my father's counsel to me was due to his own ignorance of Persian; and how if I were now to learn it unbeknown to him, I should not only surprise but delight him by coming out first in the examination. Persuaded by such arguments, I resolved to learn Persian; and that very week I began my studies, borrowing, as though I were committing some secret crime, a copy of the Tuhfe-i Vehbí [1] belonging to the school.

'I well remember that one night, before I had quite finished the Tuhfe, I was seated opposite my lala, for we were grinding wheat for bulghur [2] in a hand-mill. It came to my turn to work the mill, and as I was doing so I saw that tears were rolling from my lala's eyes; he was weeping. I asked him the reason. He replied, "You are still a child; you could not understand." I pressed him till he was forced to answer, "Do you know what that mill is saying with its silent tongue?" As up to that moment I had never heard of a mill speaking, I looked in the lala's face in bewilderment and said, "Pray tell me how the mill speaks."

'The lala heaved a deep sigh and said, "Yes, the mill speaks, and speaks far more eloquently and sensibly than we; but one needs ears to hear it. Aye, this mill is saying with its silent tongue, 'O ye heedless who look at me, open

[1] The riming Persian-Turkish vocabulary by Sunbul-záde Vehbí. See Vol. IV, pp. 257—8.

[2] Bulghur is wheat deprived of its husk by boiling and pounding; it is used in making soups and pilaws.

your eyes and look well at me, for I am a symbol of the
world. The grains that you put in me are as the men who
come into the world. Bruising these grains between two
stones, I break them and grind them small, and when they
have been brought to that state of fitness in which they
become bulghur, I cast them out and busy myself with
those that take their place. Even so does the world crush
the men who enter it with all manner of trials and sorrows
between (the stones of) earth and sky till they are made
perfect — that is, till each has received his share, — when
it casts them out into the grave and busies itself with
others. Yes, and there have occurred to me," added the lala,
"some verses to this effect." Then he improvised a few couplets
of which, alas, nothing but this line remains in my memory:

'I looked upon that Harmony which makes the mill to turn.' [1]

'As I was not of an age to understand the import of
these words, I was more impressed by my lala's talents and
accomplishments than by the mill's pretty speech, and my
desire to learn Persian and so know the meaning of the
words ásyáb and áhenk [2] was increased. Moreover, the way
in which the lala worked his eyes and eyebrows, and the
melody of the poetry, which he recited in a fashion I
understood not, [3] delighted me yet more than the meaning,
and I besought him to explain to me the poetic art. "What
they call Poetry," answered he, "is a divine gift granted to
some alone; it does not come by study and application. If
God has decreed it for you, you will be a poet; otherwise
you can never attain to that glory. Can Khoja Nuʿmán

[1] آسیابی دور ایدن او آهنگه نظر قیلمشدم

The 'Harmony' referred to is of course the Divine Scheme of things.

[2] In the lala's hemistich the Persian words ásyáb (mill) and áhenk (harmony) are used.

[3] I. e. having regard to the metre, etc.

write poetry for all that he is so profoundly learned in every science? Look at ʿÍsá Efendi; though he is unrivalled in his knowledge of Persian, has he the skill to make poetry? Poetry is the gift of God; it is not to be obtained through learning."

'No sooner had I heard this than I felt in myself an emotion as though a smouldering fire had been blown into flame within me. I could rest still no longer. I left the mill, and weeping, threw my arms about my lala's neck, and prayed him earnestly to teach me how poetry is written. The lala was a sympathetic though sad-hearted man, and he looked at me pitifully, and said in a tender voice, "Since this love and desire is in you, I believe you will be a poet." He then explained to me, so far as he himself understood it, how what is called Poetry is simply words arranged conformably to the movements and pauses of the Fáʿilátuns and Mefáʿiluns [1] which they call metres and prosody, and how it is necessary that the ends of the lines should rime together. After which he said, "As you are so eager after poetry, let your first verse be, for good luck, a hymn to the Prophet. [2] Now try to-night; make something in that manner, and show it to me to-morrow; we shall correct the places where there are mistakes; and in this way you will become a poet." And he recommended me to use as a refrain [3] the words, 'O apostle of God!' [4]

'Delighted, I mounted the stair at full speed, ran into my room, shut the door, and spread out before me a sheet of paper. I seized my pen, as though I were about to write

---

[1] Fáʿilátun and Mefáʿilun are the paradigms or meaningless model words for two of the Oriental prosodic feet. The first stands for I−◡−−I, the second for I◡−◡−I.

[2] A naʿt.   [3] Redíf.

[4] يا رسول اللّٰه.

down a crowd of things that were heaped up in my mind. Think! go on! think! — not a thing would come into my head. Where were metre and prosody? — even common words had fled from my mind as though they had feared to be taken and thrust by force into the fetters of metre. In short, I could think of absolutely nothing. And so the dawn came; I had not slept for a moment. Then saying to myself, "Let come what will," I wrote down on the paper a few lines of nonsense; but I did not forget to end each with 'O apostle of God!' I read these over a hundred times, and found them all to my own thinking correct in metre and very fine; but it never occurred to me to give any thought as to their meaning.

'As soon as it was light I ran full of joy to my lala's room and caught him performing his ablution, having just risen from bed. I thrust my paper triumphantly into his hand. He cast his eye over it, then handed it back to me and said with a smile, "This is not bad; but poetry must be metrical, that is, the movements and pauses must be equal in every line; now not only are some of these Fáᶜilátun and some Mustefᶜilun, [1] but there is no sense to be made out of any one of them. The words glare at one another like mad bulls. Now sense as well as metre is an essential of poetry. Keep these; but try to write as I told you last night, and to-morrow we shall see."

'Then I read my poem over again and saw all the faults the lala had pointed out. Who could care for lessons any longer! To become a poet was more desirable in my eyes than to be King of all the world. So I thought about poetry all that day in school; even when playing walnuts [2]

[1] This word is the paradigm of the prosodic foot I − − ∪ −I.

[2] Walnuts are used for playing many games, some of which resemble those played with marbles by boys in this country.

in the mosque courtyard I was dreaming about poetry. Again I worked hard all night till morning and managed to scribble something. Next day I showed it to the lala, and while he was glancing over it, my heart beat fast, and I looked at his eyes, wondering what he would say. I do not know whether it was to encourage me, or whether the metre and sense were really correct, or whether they seemed so to my lala, but in any case he clasped me in his arms and said, "Well done! I no longer doubt that you will be a poet; your father or whosoever will may forbid, but I no longer fear." These words fanned, as it were, the fires of eagerness in my heart. Saving up from a few days' allowances, I went secretly with my lala to the booksellers and we bought a collection of ʿAshiq ʿOmer's verses which I diligently studied in the evenings.

'I very soon began to discover which of the verses the lala used to compose and recite were out of metre, and even to make 'parallels' to the couplets I liked best in the ʿAshiq ʿOmer and Gevherí that I was reading. But I did not pay much attention to sense until I became acquainted with the late Fatín Efendi.[1] I had been fancying myself a full-fledged poet and the worshipped ʿAshiq ʿOmer an erudite master whose like had never been seen on earth when the aforesaid Efendi was the means of rectifying my errors.'

At this point the autobiographical portion of Ziyá Bey's preface ends. It was written to introduce and illustrate what follows it, a series of reflections on the education of children, the subject of Rousseau's work to the translation of which it is prefixed. There is however a section in the preface to his anthology, the oft-quoted Kharábát or Tavern, in which Ziyá describes how he came to be interested in poetry, and of which, as it supplements the story just told, I shall here

[1] The author of the Tezkire which has been so often quoted.

give a translation. The original is in verse, but for brevity's sake I shall render it in prose, omitting whatever is irrelevant.

'Before I was fifteen years of age I busied myself with verse; what first gave me the taste therefor was the braying of the street-poets.[1] Sometimes I would read Gharíbí or be stirred up by ʿAshiq Kerem;[2] at other times I would take up ʿAshiq ʿOmer and be confounded by his erotic speeches. But I was not content with admiring; sometimes I made bold to pilfer, and I would try to write 'parallels'. What productions they were! May all ears be spared hearing such things, and all lips uttering them! Yet I wrote them in my little díwán, and would, if I could, have carved them on the rocks. Whoever cast the stone of derision at my verses got himself into trouble with me, and I answered the criticiser with a satire. A year or so passed thus when I became possessed of a treasure in the shape of one or two old printed díwáns, and when I got these I entered into another world. Gevherí's slippers were now thrown aside.[3] I admired Vehbí and Wásif, and strove to imitate them. When reading I would say, 'What magic! what a miracle! Can any speech surpass this, so sweet in language, so brilliant in conception? Look at that cypress, that form and figure! How charming the connection of rose and nightingale! Surely the moth is indeed the taper's lover!" But as yet I was unable to discriminate. However, when I read the

---

[1] Literally 'public-square poets' (maydán shuʿarási) that is, men who for money sing or recite verses from the popular poets such as ʿAshiq ʿOmer in public places.

[2] Gharíbí and ʿAshiq Kerem (Kerem the Minstrel), popular poets of the type of ʿAshiq ʿOmer and Gevherí.

[3] پابوجى دامه آتلدى 'His slippers have been thrown on the roof,' is a proverbial expression meaning 'he has fallen from the high esteem in which he was held (some other having taken his place.') It is often said of a first child when a second is born. Here Ziyá would imply that his youthful allegiance was transferred from Gevherí and the folk-poets to Vehbí and Wásif.

Gulistán [1] I began to discover what language is. Just then, too, I was assisted in my studies by certain poets, [2] one of whom induced me to read a considerable part of Háfiz. My whole nature was enthralled by what I read; it was as though my closed eyes were opened. The Persian poets became my masters, and I gathered gems from many of their Khamsas and Díwáns.'

Such were the circumstances under which Ziyá's poetic talents were developed. I have given them here in detail and in the author's own words; for, apart from its personal interest, the narrative may be taken as typical. No other Ottoman poet has left a similar record, but, save that Ziyá was probably more than usually fortunate in his lala, the story which he tells was doubtless in its main outlines that of many a Turkish poet born in a non-literary family. A natural talent for poetry first awakened by the songs and rimes of the folk-poets heard in public places from the lips of ᶜáshiqs or wandering minstrels, followed by attempts at versifying modelled with more or less accuracy upon the poems in any stray díwán the young enthusiast might lay hands on, refined and corrected by intercourse with literary friends won to interest by his manifest abilities, and matured by study of the great Persian classics, — such must have been the steps by which many a Turkish poet of bygone times scaled the slopes of the national Parnassus.

In the biographical and critical notice which Ebu-z-Ziyá Tevfíq Bey has prefixed to the selections from Ziyá's prose works in his Specimens of Ottoman Literature [3] we find many interesting particulars of the poet's subsequent career.

---

[1] The famous Persian work by Sheykh Saᶜdí of Shíráz which is held as a classic throughout the East.

[2] No doubt Fatín Efendi is one of those referred to.

[3] Numúne-i Edebiyyát-i ᶜOsmániyya, edition of 1308.

The information from this source is of special value, as Tevfíq Bey was personally acquainted not only with Ziyá, but with many of that author's friends and associates. The following details may therefore be regarded as scarcely less authoritative than the story just related.

In 1262 (1846), when Ziyá Bey was some seventeen years of age, he received an appointment in the office of the Chief Secretary of the Grand Vezirate. It was very soon after he entered upon his duties at the Porte that he made the acquaintance of Fatín Efendi, to whose assistance he confesses that he owed so much. Encouraged by him and by other literary men whom he soon got to know, he worked assiduously at his poetry, producing verses which Tevfíq Bey declares to be equal, if not superior, to the best of those of his most distinguished contemporaries.

His literary efforts for the next nine years or so were directed exclusively towards poetry, and the amount of verse written by him during this period must have been considerable. Indeed his friend and counsellor ›Fatín Efendi, writing in 1271 (1854), says that by that time Ziyá had composed ghazels enough to form a díwán. But all this work was in the old style, chiefly in the then fashionable manner of the ʿArif Hikmet group, so that what has been preserved of it is now of little account, having been altogether eclipsed by the far more original ̀and brilliant work which the poet produced later on under the influence of the new learning.

During these nine years when Ziyá Bey was employed at the Porte and was exercising his poetic talent in the production of Neo-Persianist verses, he was leading a wild and gay, not to say dissolute, life. This was perhaps inevitable, seeing that it was in the taverns and other places of debauchery where drinking-parties used to be held that the young poets of those days made their rendezvous. 'Alas!' cries Tevfíq Bey, 'some of those who used to frequent those rendezvous have since roamed the wastes of madness, [1] while others still in their youth have been snatched away by the hand of death.' Tevfíq Bey then mentions as being of the number of these unhappy ones, whom he never saw, but whose sad story he heard from their boon-companions, Háfiz Mushfiq and ʿAlí; while amongst those whom he himself had met were Ghálib and Hálet Beys and Emín Firdevsí. [2] But whether it was that he possessed a stronger constitution, or that he had the good sense to temper self-indulgence with moderation, Ziyá Bey, although he associated with such men as these and shared in their merry-makings and dissipations, escaped the untoward fate by which so many among them were overtaken.

Yet this same Ziyá Bey, who spent his nights in the tavern carousing with his boon-companions, passed his days in his office at the Porte, where, owing partly to his self-reliance and partly to his ambition to outstrip his colleagues,

---

[1] This perhaps refers to the poet Haqqí who went mad.

[2] The men whose names Tevfíq Bey mentions here as being among Ziyá's gay companions were mostly journalists connected with the Jeríde-i Hawádis, the well-known Turkish semi-official newspaper. Háfiz Mushfiq was born in Constantinople in 1221 (1806-7), and is said to have known the Koran by heart when eight years old. He was in the Civil Service, was for a time editor of the Jeríde, and wrote a volume which he called Mushfiq-náme, the Book of Mushfiq (i. e. of the Compassionate one). ʿAlí Efendi, who was likewise a native of Constantinople, was also in the Civil Service, and at one time edited the Jeríde. The Ghálib Bey referred to is probably the poet who is generally known as Lesqofchali Ghálib Bey. Hálet Bey was born in 1255 (1837—40) and when quite young contributed to the Jeríde. He was in Aleppo when the local official journal Furát, The Euphrates, was started, whereon he brought out a private paper which he called Ghadír-ul-Furát, The Pool of the Euphrates. When he returned to Constantinople he started a literary magazine called Doláb, The Cupboard. He wrote a life of Fuʾád Pasha, also a volume of poems entitled Hálet-ush-Shebáb, The World of Youth. He died in 1295 (1878).

he soon made his way and attracted general attention. His devil-may-care airs, his dissolute life, his familiarity with disreputable characters, the satires and lampoons which he launched against high and low, — all were notorious; but so keen was his intelligence and so brilliant were his talents that everything besides was overlooked. His colleagues in the Chief Secretary's office, when they saw the extraordinary ease and grace with which he composed in that highly elaborated and wonderfully involved official style — to write in which was sore travail to even the oldest of his fellow-clerks, — were, whether they would or no, constrained to acknowledge and admire his marvellous ability.

For all this, Ziyá made no money by his pen; his father's purse had to provide for all, from the clothes upon his back to the expenses of his nightly revels.[1] This, however, gave but little concern to the young Bey, all of whose serious efforts were directed to the increase and advancement of his own culture. The way in which he set about accomplishing this may at first sight seem peculiar; but we must remember how, as Tevfíq Bey points out, it was in the taverns that the more brilliant of the younger literary men of those days were in the habit of holding their symposia, and how consequently it was thither he who would share the pleasure or advantage of their society must go. 'We too', continues the biographer, 'have our Gümüsh-Halqali (Silver-Ring), our Servili (Cypress-Inn), and our Altun-Uluq (Golden-Spout),[2] cabarets which are now looked upon as places of historic interest, even as the Café Procope, the Café Molière or the Chat-Noir in Paris, once the resorts of Molière,

---

[1] It should be mentioned to Ziyá's credit that after he had 'ranged himself' he set about repaying his father with interest all the money which he had caused him to disburse.

[2] These are the names of taverns frequented by Ziyá and his friends.

Piron, Voltaire, Diderot, Mirabeau and other men of letters.'
In one or other of these Constantinople taverns, according
to the season, met the wits and poets of those times, and
while the glasses were going round some one would recite
a ghazel of Háfiz or criticise a couplet of Feyzí, or some
other would declaim a ghazel composed by himself in the
manner of Fuzúlí or a few verses from a qasída written
after the fashion of Nefⁱí.

Things went on in this way till the year 1271 (1854—5),
when Ziyá Bey was, through the influence of Reshíd Pasha,
appointed third secretary to the Sultan. Ziyá's wonderful
skill in secretarial work, as well as his poetic talent, had
come under the notice of Reshíd Pasha and the Sheykh-ul-
Islám ᶜArif Hikmet Bey; and the former, who was then
Grand Vezír, wishing to promote the interests of so promising
a young man, procured for him the above-mentioned office
in the Imperial household. From the day he entered the
Sultan's palace Ziyá began a new life; he felt that he owed
the honourable position in which he found himself neither
to his birth nor to any favouritism, but to his own merit
and talent alone, and he determined that he would do what
in him lay to maintain and increase his fair fame. He therefore turned his back on his former life, gave up his Bohemian
companions, and set himself to walk in the straight way as
became a dignified and learned member of so august a
household.

But so sudden and violent a break from habits of long
standing could hardly be effected with absolute impunity;
a kind of mental paralysis seemed to come over the young
man; the Ziyá who used to sing 'like a nightingale' amongst
his jovial friends seated on the bare benches of some dingy,
grimy little tavern, moved silent as a mute through the
gilded saloons of the Imperial palace. Edhem Pasha, the

then marshal of the Sultan's household, noticed the depression of Ziyá Bey, and strongly urged him to seek relief from it by turning his attention to the study of French. The Bey followed this advice, and, devoting all his energies to this new pursuit, acquired in six months so good a knowledge of the French language that he was able to translate into Turkish an historical treatise by Viardot on the Moors in Spain. This work, the Turkish title of which is Endelus Táríkhi, The History of Andalusia, is the first of Ziyá's prose productions important from a literary point of view. Of course, the evidences of the translator's training are apparent in every sentence. The style has more affinity with the bureaucratic idiom of the Sublime Porte than with the simple and graceful manner of the translator's maturer works. Not even a Ziyá Bey could at once master a foreign language and evolve a new literary style in the brief space of six months.

For several years Ziyá retained his position in the Imperial household, and during the whole time he worked continuously at his French studies, translating numerous books, and ever seeking to make for himself a more and more perfect literary style, by assimilating and applying those principles which he recognised as lying at the foundations of the idiom and the literature that he was studying. There is nothing to indicate that in so doing Ziyá was in any way influenced by the very similar efforts that were then being made by Shinásí. The two reformers appear, independently of one another, to have attacked the same problem with the same weapons at very nearly the same time, a not unnatural occurrence under the circumstances, and one which confirms what has been said as to the inevitableness of the rise of the Modern School in Ottoman literature at this particular juncture.

Amongst the French works mentioned as having been translated by Ziyá during these years are Molière's 'Tartufe', a 'History of the Inquisition', Fénelon's 'Télémaque', and La Fontaine's 'Fables', the last being rendered into verse. But as there was little demand for such literature in those days, these works remained unpublished, and with the exceptions of the 'Tartufe' [1] and the 'History of the Inquisition', [2] which were issued shortly after the translator's death, they appear to have been lost. The translation of Rousseau's 'Emil' is probably later; at least the preface, a part of which we have just read, is dated 15th Muharrem 1287 (April 1870), and was written at Geneva where Ziyá was then living in quasi-exile.

Although so busy with prose, Ziyá was not neglecting poetry. A large number of his lyric poems, including the best known of all, a Terjíᶜ-bend, were written during his tenure of office in the Palace. The effects of the author's European studies are very noticeable in these verses, alike in the clarity and directness of the thought and in the relative simplicity and sobriety of the expression. The outlook on life, too, is Western rather than Eastern, though the external form and mechanism of the verse remains Oriental throughout.

[1] Ziyá's translation of the 'Tartufe' is entitled Riyániñ Enjámi 'The Result of Hypocrisy', and was issued in 1298 (1881), the year after his death, from the printing-office of the Waqt newspaper. It is rendered literally, line for line, in a kind of blank verse without regular rime or metre. The printed edition begins abruptly in the middle of the sixth scene of the first act. Perhaps the first few pages of the manuscript were lost.

[2] The Inkizisyon Táríkhi or 'History of the Inquisition' was published in 1299 (1882) by Ebu-z-Ziyá Tevfíq Bey, who says in a prefatory note that the translation was made twenty-two years ago, and that on the author's death his heirs, who were ignorant of its real value, sold the manuscript at Adana for a quarter mejídiyye (about one shilling), and that he, unwilling that the public should be deprived of a precious work by so great an author, bought the manuscript for four hundred times the price at which it had been sold, and published it.

The story of Ziyá's later life cannot be given here in any detail. The materials out of which to form it have not yet been published, nor are they likely to be under the present repressive régime; for the Bey became one of the most prominent members of the Young Turkey party, no word concerning which is allowed to issue from the Ottoman press.

Some time after the accession of ʿAbd-ul-ʿAzíz, which occurred in 1277 (June 1861), the Bey ceased to be a member of the Imperial household. This change was in all probability a result of the hostility which existed between him and ʿAlí Pasha, whose influence had become all powerful with the new Sultan. ʿAlí and his colleague Fuʾád Pasha had, as we have seen, been the rivals of Reshíd Pasha and the persecutors of Shinásí, and Ziyá bitterly resented the growing power of the former. He had more than once tried to bring about the fall of his enemy by representing to Sultan ʿAbd-ul-ʿAzíz how ʿAlí was in reality usurping the imperial power, a proceeding which naturally roused the resentment of the Pasha, and eventually entailed the dismissal of Ziyá from his position as secretary to the Sultan.

After his removal from the Palace, Ziyá was appointed to a succession of more or less nominal offices; and it was during this time that he, in conjunction with several of the better educated and more talented of his younger contemporaries, laid the foundations of the Young Turkey party. These young men, among the most prominent of whom was Kemál Bey, had begun to realise the unhappy and backward state of their country, and were filled with an overmastering desire to do something to bring about a brighter and better state of things. Their aim was the regeneration of Turkey and her establishment as one of the great civilised powers of the world. Among the most important of the means by which they sought to accomplish this end was an idea, at first not very clearly defined, of substituting for the absolute despotism which had hitherto prevailed a constitutional régime under which the Sultan should rule conjointly with a parliament duly elected from all the nationalities within the Empire. The reformers flooded Constantinople and the provinces with tracts and pamphlets setting forth their views and drawing attention to the evils of the existing system. This brought them into collision with Ziyá's old enemy, the then all-powerful Grand Vezír ʿAlí Pasha, who, although sincerely desirous of the welfare of the country, did not approve of the revolutionary schemes of the reformers, holding that such reforms as were made must be compatible with the principle of absolute monarchy which was in harmony with the genius of the East. Hoping therefore to check the new movement and nip in the bud any aspirations after Freedom, as that word was understood in the West, he thought to break up the party by banishing under one pretext or another its leading spirits from the capital and scattering them in remote provinces. A large number of suspected persons were thus got rid of in the spring and summer of 1867.

Ziyá was naturally amongst those singled out for banishment; and so he received the titular appointment of Governor of Cyprus, but before he could be shipped off to Famagusta, where he believed he would be secretly poisoned, he contrived to elude the authorities and escape to Europe along with his colleagues Kemál, Núrí and Rifʿat Beys, and ʿAlí Suʿáví Efendi. This took place at the beginning of the year 1284, that is, in the early summer of 1867.

Some at least of the refugees who at this time made their escape to Europe had been invited by the Egyptian Prince, Mustafá Fázil Pasha, to join him in Paris, whither he had fled from Constantinople some little time before on account of a quarrel betv/een himself and ʿAlí Pasha. Until June 1866, when the direct succession to the Viceroyalty was granted by the Sultan, Mustafá Fázil had been the heir to the viceregal throne, and this alteration of the law, which resulted in his exclusion from his hereditary rights, had naturally incensed him against its authors. In order to carry out his scheme of revenge by attacking the Imperial government through the press, he desired to have with him in Europe some able Turkish writers who were opposed to the Grand Vezír and the system he represented. Hence his invitation to the leaders of the Young Turkey party. The Prince was enormously wealthy, and he promised to maintain as long as they lived those men who came to Europe at his request, a promise which he soon afterwards broke, as ere long he made his peace with the Ottoman court, and, leaving his protégés to shift for themselves as best they could, returned to Constantinople where he was reinstated in high favour, — for all of which he is bitterly reproached by Ziyá in his famous satire called the Zafer-náme.

After a time Ziyá and his companions found it advisable to move their camp from Paris to London, which city they accordingly made their head-quarters. While in the West they brought out two Turkish newspapers, named respectively, the Mukhbir or 'Correspondent' and the Hurriyyet or 'Liberty'.[1] In these papers, very many copies of which were smuggled into Turkey, they continued their propaganda in favour of a limited monarchy and representative government; and many of the articles contributed by Kemál and Ziyá were most ably and eloquently written.

From London Ziyá went to Geneva, where he was in

[1] In 1894 the Hurriyyet was revived in London in the interest of the Ottoman constitutional party under the editorship of 'Djiwanpire' (Juván-pír), i. e. Selím Fáris Efendi.

the spring of 1870, and whence, as we have seen, he dated the preface to his translation of 'Emil'. About this time the fugitivés who had been pardoned by the Sultan for their unceremonious departure began to return singly to Constantinople; but Ziyá did not dare to set foot in Turkey so long as his enemy ᶜAlí Pasha lived. At length, however, in 1288 (September 1871), the Grand Vezír died, whereupon Ziyá adressed to the Sultan a qasída in which, after praising him in the conventional extravagant and fulsome manner, he apologises for his flight, which, he says, was exclusively due to the rancour of an enemy who sought to banish him to Cyprus in order to kill him there, and humbly craves the Imperial pardon. Although it is not likely that Ziyá's palinode had much effect on Sultan ᶜAbd-ul-ᶜAzíz, his prayer was granted, and he shortly afterwards received the much-desired permission to return.

Back in his native country, Ziyá was once more enrolled in the government service, being employed, after the fashion of the Porte, now in one capacity and now in another. His leisure was given to the compilation of his great anthology, the often-mentioned Kharábát or 'Tavern', the publication of the three volumes of which extended from 1291 (1874—5) to 1292 (1875—6).

On the accession of Sultan ᶜAbd-ul-Hamíd in Shaᶜbán 1293 (August 1876), Ziyá Bey was promoted to the rank of Vezír, and so acquired the title of Pasha, whence it has been usual to speak of him since then as Ziyá Pasha. At the same time he was nominated governor of Syria, the suspicious and nervous monarch who now occupied the throne wishing, perhaps, to get one who had been so intimately connected with the constitutional party removed to a safe distance from the capital. Like Kemál, Ziyá was not permitted to stand as a candidate for the Parliament to the creation of which his influence had so greatly contributed. From Syria Ziyá Pasha was transferred to Qonya, and from Qonya to Adana, where he died early in the Latter Jemází of 1297 (May 1880), worn with disease and broken-hearted at what he deemed the failure of his life-work.

Ziyá Pasha is described by his friend Ebu-z-Ziyá Tevfíq Bey as having been a brilliant conversationalist and delightful companion, gifted with a great command of language, a ready wit and a keen sense of humour.

Besides the translations from the French already referred to, Ziyá wrote in prose a number of articles and treatises on various political and social questions. In such of these as were produced after he had perfected his style, we find an ease and an absence of visible effort such as Shinásí never attained. Shinásí set out upon his work as reformer with greater earnestness of purpose, Ziyá with greater brilliancy of native talent. The superiority of the purely literary gift of the latter is beyond question, and should it be asked how Shinásí and not Ziyá has come to be regarded by the modern writers as the founder of their school, the answer must be sought in the all-powerful influence of Kemál Bey. It was the extraordinary literary genius and unvarying loftiness of purpose of that great writer — by many held to be the greatest Turkey has ever known — that brought about the wonderfully swift and complete success of the Modern School; and all Kemál's contemporaries and successors have ever been at one in looking up to him as their master and their greatest glory. Now Kemál was the disciple of Shinásí, the inspiring influence of whose precept and example he never lost an opportunity of gratefully acknowledging. Ziyá, on the other hand, became known to Kemál only later on, and then not as teacher but as fellow-worker. Kemál is the chief captain of the Moderns, Shinásí was the guide and inspirer of Kemál; therefore Shinásí, and not another, is honoured as the founder.

Unlike Shinásí, Ziyá was a born poet. His earlier productions, the verses that he wrote before entering the Imperial household, were, as has been said, in the current fashion of the day, that is in the manner of ʿArif Hikmet and his school. His old friend Fatín Efendi mentions him with praise in his Tezkire, but as that work was published in 1271 (1854), before the poet had well passed his salad days, the notice it contains is necessarily confined to this immature work. Fatín however mentions two productions which I have seen noticed nowhere else; these are a riming Persian-Turkish vocabulary written as a 'parallel' to Vehbí's Tuhfe, and a commentary to an Arabic Tuhfe by ʿAsim Efendi the famous translator of the Qámús and the Burhán-i Qátiʿ. The biographer states further that his young friend had written a series of supplementary articles to the then recently published 'Ottoman Grammar' of Jevdet and Fuʾád Efendis.

The best of Ziyá's lyric work was produced between the years 1271 (1854—5), when he became secretary to the Sultan, and 1284 (1867) when he fled to Europe. The verses written during this period, after the poet had made some acquaintance with French literature, are of great interest as presenting the earliest examples of Turkish poetry produced under the direct influence of Western culture. In the best known of all, the very remarkable Terjíʿ-bend which Ziyá wrote in 1276 (1859), the inspiration is wholly Western. It is the spirit of Western agnosticism that breathes throughout this poem; it is Western science that has revealed to the poet those mysteries at which he stands aghast; the attitude of his mind before the terrible problem faced is not that of the Muhammedan thinker, nor yet of the dervish mystic, it is that of the European of the nineteenth century.

And so in most of the poems written about this time we can see in one form or another traces of the author's Occidental studies. In the past the general tendency had been to consider poetry either as a sort of intellectual plaything or as a medium for the expression of transcendental ideas. Ziyá thought to bring it more into harmony with modern life by employing it, much as he employed prose, as a vehicle for expressing what he, a man of the world and no mystic, regarded as practically the truth. The French poets had taught him that serious and earnest poetry might be written without flying off into the regions of mysticism, that the hopes and fears common to all men, if treated with sympathy and sincerity, would yield material for the noblest efforts of genius. Ziyá's lyrics, then, differ widely in purpose from those of most of his contemporaries and predecessors; there is little attempt at prettiness, still less at transcendentalism;[1] his object is to state things as he believes them to be, and to give voice to his own views regarding them. In his attempts, however, to avoid the futilities of the 'Arif Hikmets on the one hand and the enigmas of the Esrár Dedes on the other, he at times stumbles into yet a third ditch. So great is his respect for common-sense that sometimes his verses are little else than rather ordinary prose thrown into metrical form. The language of these poems is in keeping with their substance, simple and straightforward on the whole, with little that is merely decorative, nothing that is wilfully obscure.

Although the pervading spirit is Western, the imagery remains Oriental. It is the same with the external form; there is no attempt at any innovation in the mechanism of

[1] So far as I have seen, it is only in the hymn which opens the preface to the Kharábát that there is any trace of the dervish mysticism in Ziyá's poetry.

verse. Ziyá's Díwán contains nothing but what is quite orthodox, — qasída and ghazel, terjíᶜ and sharqí, all as in the past. The next step, the introduction into Turkish poetry of European verse-forms and rime-schemes was reserved for another and a greater than Ziyá.

While inspired by the genius of the West, Ziyá's work is never an imitation of European poetry; he did not attempt to write French poetry in Turkish words, as did certain of his successors, who thus unconsciously walked in the footsteps of those ancestors of theirs whose aim had been to manufacture Persian poetry out of the same materials. These poems of Ziyá are the expression of a mind which, without ceasing to be, or seeking to cease to be, essentially Oriental, has been open to the influences of European culture. And in this respect they are unique; what has gone before has been exclusively Eastern, while from that which follows the Oriental element has been in great part deliberately eliminated. Ziyá's Díwán forms the link between the purely Asiatic work of the Old School and the Europe-inspired poetry of the Modern. It might be taken either as the last word of the former or as the first word of the latter. The qasídas alone are wholly Eastern, and these form the least important section of the Díwán, being neither better nor worse than hundreds of their kind.

When I spoke in a previous chapter of Ziyá's poetry being in an eminent degree typical of the twenty years between 1859 and 1879, it was more especially this Díwán that was present in my mind; for in it more particularly we feel that the author is struggling to deal with modern themes, yet can find no means of utterance but that of the by-gone generations.

No edition of Ziyá's lyric poems was published during his life-time; but in 1298 (1881), a year after his death, a

selection of these edited by his brother-in-law Commander
Hamdí Bey was brought out under the title of Esh'ár-i
Ziyá or 'Poems of Ziyá.' It is this selection which I have
spoken of as the 'Díwán'; but the author has very many
poems not included therein. Some of these are to be found
in his own anthology the Kharábát; but the majority, especially those that touch on political affairs, have never been
printed and still circulate in manuscript alone.

Among the best known of these prescribed poems is one
which, according to the story, was found among the author's
papers after his death. In form this too is a terjí'-bend,
which, like the poet's earlier work of the same class, is pes-
simistic in tone. But here the note is more personal. Ziyá
Pasha died in the belief that the great work to which he
had devoted his life and his splendid talents had ended in
hopeless failure. He had worked hard and suffered much in
his country's cause; and now at the end he saw the old
evil Byzantinism again triumphant, and the infant constitution
strangled by despotic hands; while the champions of liberty,
slain, imprisoned, or, like himself, in virtual exile, were power-
less to strike one blow or raise one cry on behalf of freedom.
And the people — the people for whose sake they had
toiled so hard and borne so much — stood still and did
nothing. Instincts born of centuries of unquestioning submission to a ruler's will were not to be wholly done away
by a brief propaganda, however earnest and gifted might
be the preachers; but Ziyá, disappointed in his dearest hopes
and racked with suffering physical and mental, thought not
of this, nor had he faith to foresee that the seed which he
had sown would yet ere many years were past bear a rich
and abundant harvest. And so he arose and with almost
his dying breath denounced his people and his country, and
anathematised his own efforts made to save them.

'Naught but sorrows on the loyal to this Empire ever wait;
'Sheerest madness is devotion to this People and this State.'

Such is the refrain of what is probably the saddest poem
in the Turkish language.

In many respects the most remarkable of all Ziyá's writings
is his famous satire the Zafer-Náme. This work stands by
itself in Ottoman literature; there is nothing the least like
it in the past, and as yet no one has attempted to imitate
it. Several of the earlier poets, it is true, wrote what they
were pleased to regard as satires; but the verses of this
class composed by such men as Nef'í and Surúrí are little
else than strings of grossly abusive epithets, exercises in
vulgar vituperation, the grotesque abominations of which
serve only to disgust the reader with their foul-mouthed
authors. The work of Ziyá is very different; the Zafer-Náme
is really a satire as that term is understood in modern
Europe. Although it is not quite free from personal allusions,
which are at times in somewhat dubious taste, there is no
trace, however faint, of the outrageous scurrility of the 'Shafts
of Doom'; the poet seeks his purpose either through bitterly
ironical praise of his victim, or by holding up to ridicule
his pretentious ignorance. Here again the influence of the
West is evident; had Ziyá known nothing of French literature,
the Zafer-Náme would either never have been written, or
it would have been quite other than it is.

The satire is directed against the political enemies of the
Young Turkey party, who for the most part were also the
personal enemies of the author. While the chief victim is,
of course, the Grand Vezír 'Alí Pasha, many of his colleagues
and flatterers, notably Fu'ád Pasha, are incidentally attacked.
The name Zafer-Náme or 'Book of Victory', (we might
translate it as 'The Pæan',) which is a very common title
in old Turkish and Persian literature for an account, in

either prose or verse, of the military triumphs of some great warrior or monarch, was chosen by Ziyá on account of the irony of its suggestiveness. The poem which he so called is in form a qasída, and is composed in a strain of the most exaggerated and bombastic eulogy. Its ostensible object, and that to which it owes its name, is the celebration of the Grand Vezír's expedition to Crete in the autumn of 1867 in order to bring to a close the rebellion which had for some time been devastating that island; but its scope is really much wider, the whole of the Vezír's policy being passed in review, always in the same tone of ridiculously extravagant laudation.

The satire would have lost much of its point had Ziyá avowedly written it himself; he therefore attributes it to one of ʿAlí Pasha's warmest partisans, Fázil Pasha the Bosnian, who was then mutesarrif or governor of Izmid. In thus making him the author of this absurd panegyric on his patron, Ziyá deals a by-thrust at the old Bosnian, with whom he had a crow to pluck. For when the reformers fled from Constantinople, this Fázil, wishing yet further to ingratiate himself with ʿAlí Pasha, had written some verses on the subject which, if we are to believe Ziyá, so pleased the infuriated Vezir that he straightway appointed the writer mutesarrif of Izmid.

But the Zafer-Náme qasída by no means completes the satire; in order to reinforce his attack on ʿAlí Pasha, and at the same time to wing a shaft against another adversary, Ziyá wrote a takhmís on the qasída, which he attributed to Khayrí Efendi, a retired employé of the quarantine department. Even this was not enough; the satirist crowns the whole by a prose commentary on the qasída thus turned into a mukhammes, which he fathers on an adversary to whom he owed a very special grudge, Husní Pasha, ʿAlí's

Marshal of Police.[1] In this extraordinary production Ziyá pushes home ruthlessly and relentlessly his attack alike on ʿAlí and Fuʾád Pashas, on Fázil, Khayrí, and Husní, as well as on a host of minor foes.

Fázil, Khayrí and Husní had all three dabbled in poetry, hence the appropriateness of the ascription to them of the three parts of the mock-eulogy. This ascription was not made by Ziyá with the least intention that it should be credited; still less was it prompted by any notion of screening himself, for when he wrote the work he was safe in Europe, far beyond the reach of any adversary. The threefold attribution not only enabled him to hold up to ridicule the three fictitious authors, but heightened the whole effect of his work by imparting to it an air of verisimilitude which would otherwise have been lacking.

In conformity with their feigned authorship, qasída, takhmís, and commentary are all written in the old style, or rather in the old style travestied. But while the first two, that is the verse portions of the satire, are presented as the work of men who, though they may be shameless flatterers and very mediocre poets, are at least educated, as education was understood in the school to which they belonged, the prose commentary, on the other hand, displays its supposititious author not only as a bare-faced sycophant, but as a ridiculously pretentious and grossly illiterate clown.

The Qasída consists of sixty-six couplets, which, when the poem is extended into a mukhammes, give as many five-line stanzas. The first dozen of these are taken up with the mock-heroic panegyric on ʿAlí Pasha's doings in Crete. This is followed by an ironical eulogy of the Grand Vezir's literary skill, notably as shown in the report which he

---

[1] Zabtiyye Mushíri.

presented to the Sultan on his return from the Cretan expedition. This again leads to a consideration of the Pasha's other accomplishments, which, in its turn, opens the way to a review of the whole of ʿAlí's past policy, more especially of the various financial arrangements that he made, and of his dealings with the several foreign and quasi-foreign questions that arose between 1860 and 1868. References to a number of personal matters follow, and the poem is wound up, in imitation of the orthodox usage, with a kind of burlesque prayer for the continuance of the great man's prosperity and welfare.

Even cleverer than the verse, and certainly far more amusing, is the prose commentary. Here Ziyá had a much wider field for the exercise of his talents, and he availed himself of the opportunity to produce what is probably the wittiest piece of writing in Turkish literature. It is of considerable length, as Husní Pasha is made to follow the time-honoured practice of the Eastern commentator, who takes stanza by stanza, explaining first the individual words in each, with continual digressions more or less relevant, and then giving an explanatory paraphrase of the complete verse. This method of elucidation applied to the sixty-six stanzas of the mukhammes occupies 125 out of the 135 pages of which the lithographed edition of the satire consists. It is therefore impossible to give more than a succinct account of it here; but some further idea of certain of its features may be gained from the portions incorporated in the notes to the translated extracts from the poem.

Husní Pasha, the nominal author, was, as has been said, Marshal of Police when the Zafer-Náme was written. He had much to do with the repressive measures adopted by the Government to check the new political movement, and was consequently in exceptionally bad repute with the would-be reformers. He seems to have been a typical official of the old style, probably without much culture, possibly without too many scruples; but he can hardly have been so amazingly ignorant as he is represented, else ʿAlí Pasha would scarcely have placed him in so important a position.

In a preface which is prefixed to the commentary proper Husní Pasha is made to say, after a kind of parody on the usual introductory doxologies, that ever since his childish days he has been a devoted student of poetry, especially of the priceless works of ʿAshiq ʿOmer and Gevherí,[1] and that he has himself composed some little songs and ballads.[2] He then goes on in a comically colloquial style to give a quaintly naïve account of his career as an official and of the way in which he came to be appointed to his present position.

'The first instructions,' he proceeds, 'that I received on being appointed to this honourable office (i. e. the Marshalship of Police) were to take means to prevent the circulation in Constantinople of papers like the Hurriyyet, the Mukhbir, and the ʿUlúm[3] published by the pestilent society called the 'New Turks',[4] which had for some time dared to disturb the peace and repose of our lord ʿAlí Pasha by their seditious publications. So, putting my trust in God, I tucked up my trousers[5] and with or without right (may God pardon what

---

[1] The folk-poets mentioned on pp. 46 and 51 *supra*.

[2] In M. Belin's notice of the Turkish books published in Constantinople in 1289 (1872—3) occurs the entry: 'حسني منظومه, Poésies de Husni pacha, ancien ministre de police.' I have been unable to procure a copy of this book.

[3] The Hurriyyet and Mukhbir have been already mentioned. The ʿUlúm was a literary and scientific paper edited by Suʿávi Efendi.

[4] The 'new Turks' i. e. the members of the Young Turkey party.

[5] Pachalarini sighamaq 'to tuck up the legs of one's trousers,' is a colloquial phrase meaning to prepare to set about some important business.

I did amiss!) I imprisoned some of those connected with the leaders of this society, while some I sent into exile. When they were being examined, I could not restrain myself for my anger, and cursed and swore at every one of them like a street rough. I gave much money to spies and agents whom I found amongst the Greeks, and multiplied detectives beyond what was required; and though in view of the present state of the treasury this useless expenditure may be deplored, yet, in accordance with the saying 'necessity maketh lawful the forbidden,'[1] my heart could grudge nothing, since the peace of the inspired mind of my bounteous benefactor was dependent on the accomplishment of this serious business. Yet the miscreants still found a thousand ways and means to smuggle their papers into Constantinople; and so my heart bleeds for that while I have been the object of so much boundless favour and kindness, I have up till now been unable to perform this important service which would be acceptable to His Highness.

'Now the other day the Zafer-Náme which my brother[2] Fázil Pasha, the ex-governor of Izmid, has versified upon the Cretan victory came into my hands. A thousand times I read it, laying it down and taking it up again, and I was amazed at its eloquence and beauty of style. Then I saw the graceful takhmís which Khayrí Efendi, the retired quarantine secretary, has composed on that delightful poem, and I was so impressed by the pearls of rare words and the lustres of strange fancies that it contains that the dungeon of my desolate heart was filled with the rays of desire and zeal and enthusiasm. And I said to myself: 'That fool of a Bosniac,

---

[1] الضَّرُورَاتُ تُبِيحُ ٱلْمَحْظُورَاتِ A well-known Arabic phrase equivalent to 'necessity knows no law.'

[2] I. e. my dear friend, or my colleague.

Fázil Pasha, showed his devotion to the vezirial throne by yon qit‘a he composed when Ziyá Bey went to Europe, and thereby obtained the governorship of Izmid; Khayrí too, though fit for nothing, while sitting at home with a pension of 5,000 piastres, praying God for the prosperity of His Highness the Grand Vezír, gave proof of his claim to clientship by making a chronogram on the departure of Ziyá Bey and Kemál Bey and Su‘ávi Efendi; yet I, who, though unworthy, have, through the special favour of that lofty-purposed one, [1] obtained this rank and this office, and who am, moreover, amongst the illustrious poets of the age and formerly wrote a commentary on Ziyá Bey's terjí‘-bend, I sit still, as though now I could do nothing! What assishness is this!'

And so the Pasha, determined not to be behindhand, resolves to write a commentary on this poem in praise of his illustrious patron.

In the commentary on the first few stanzas Ziyá's object is to hold up to ridicule the crass ignorance of the nominal writer. Thus, whenever any somewhat unusual Arabic or Persian word occurs, acquaintance with which would imply some little culture, Husní is supposed to turn up his Qámús or Burhán, when out of the several meanings shown in the dictionary he invariably selects a wrong one, so that when he comes to the paraphrase of the stanza he writes the most ludicrous nonsense, which has not the slightest resemblance to the real meaning. But Ziyá soon leaves off this fooling, persistence in which would have grown wearisome, and begins to use the commentary as a channel for the indirect expression of his own views. The language, indeed, continues uncouth, is sometimes even gross, such as the real author deemed appropriate for the mouth of the feigned; things are still put in a whimsical fashion, and laughable

[1] I. e. ‘Alí Pasha.

blunders yet occur from time to time, but these are only incidental, and never intrude where they can affect the meaning of the passage; it is now Ziyá himself who is speaking through the voice of Husní. The commentary is a very skilful device to enable the satirist to extend his attack; in the mukhammes, owing to inherent limitations, only ʿAlí and Fuʾád Pashas and the two fictitious authors are directly assailed, but in the prose part of the work, where there are no such limitations, not only is the attack on the two most prominent victims renewed and driven home, but a number of other more or less important persons, including the Egyptian Mustafá Fázil Pasha, are brought under the lash, while Husní, the tool of the oppressor, is gibbeted for ever as the type of ignorant and brutal officialdom.

That the chastisement meted out by Ziyá in this satire was on the whole well-deserved may be allowed, but at the same time it is impossible to deny that he is on occasions very unfair to ʿAlí Pasha. Apart from the bad taste displayed in twitting him with his humble origin and his short stature, it is preposterous to lay to his charge all the misfortunes that befell the Empire while he was connected with the government. Ziyá Bey knew perfectly well that many of the unfortunate arrangements to which he alludes were none of the Vezir's choosing, but that he was bullied into them by the European ambassadors; and in upbraiding him with these, the poet only weakens his otherwise powerful satire.

It must, on the other hand, be remembered that if Ziyá sometimes lets his resentment get the better of his judgment, it was owing to ʿAlí Pasha that he was then an exile, that ʿAlí Pasha was his bitter personal enemy and the determined opponent of constitutional government in which, as the author truly saw, lay the only hope for his country.

The Zafer Náme is not to be criticised as poetry; the

greater part of the work is in prose, while what is in verse is purposely exaggerated to the point of becoming absurd; but it is the one great satire in Turkish literature.

The date of the composition of the work is nowhere given; but a reference in the commentary to Fu'ád Pasha as having died 'last year' enables us to fix it as 1286 (13 April 1869 — 3 April 1870).

As might be expected, the circulation of the Zafer-Náme is, and always has been, prohibited in Turkey; lithographed copies are, however, none the less easily procurable.

The last volume of the Kharábát or Tavern, the great Turkish, Persian and Arabic anthology compiled by Ziyá after his return from Europe, was published just four years before the true Modern School of Turkish poetry was inaugurated by the appearance of Hámid Bey's Sahrá. This work of Ziyá marks the last endeavour of the old Asiatic culture to retain what was left of its ancient supremacy in Ottoman literature. Never again can the dead past be held up, as it is here, as the model to which the living present must conform. But for this final effort all the forces of re-action are mustered. Side by side with what the anthologist held to be the most brilliant examples of Turkish poetry from the Birth-Song of Suleymán Chelebi down to his own Díwán, these are here presented to the young Ottoman poet, to evoke his admiring fealty and incite him to emulation, those famous and glorious masterpieces of the old Arabian and Persian classics which his fathers had ever regarded as the topmost pinnacles in the temple of human speech, the matchless paragons to approach which must be the aim of every poet. But all was in vain; 'when comes the true, the false departs,'[1] and this last barrier raised by a once mighty

---

[1] Kor'án xvii, 83: — جَاءَ ٱلْحَقُّ وَ ذَهَقَ ٱلْبَاطِلُ.

but now dying spirit fell almost without a struggle before the destructive criticism of Kemál and the creative genius of Hámid.

That Ziyá the reformer, Ziyá the satirist of the Zafer-Náme, should appear as a champion of the moribund past may seem strange; but it must be borne in mind, firstly that Ziyá had by this time lost much of his old energy, and secondly that he does not set himself up as a defender of the Old School of poetry against the New, which latter indeed was not yet in existence. If Ziyá was to make an anthology at all, it must necessarily. be compiled from the works of the Old School; yet the making of such at this juncture and the offering of it as a textbook to young poets was in fact, if not in intention, a defence of the Asiatic School.

The work consists of three volumes, the first of which was published in 1291 (1874-5), and the remaining two in the following year. The first volume contains the long and elaborate preface in mesneví verse, and the selection of Qasídas, those in Turkish coming first, arranged in ·the alphabetical order of the poets' names, those in Persian following, while those in Arabic come last. The second volume consists likewise of three parts, Turkish, Persian and Arabic, each of which is divided into several sections, as follows: Terkíb-Bends and Terjíʿ-Bends (including Mukhammeses and Museddeses), Qitʿas, Rubáʿís, Ghazels and selected couplets from such. The third volume contains extracts from famous Mesnevís, in two parts, Turkish and Persian.

The preface to the Kharábát is very interesting. It opens, according to old custom, with a hymn to God followed by one in honour of the Prophet. Then comes the 'Reason of the Compilation.' This begins with the writer's account of his early interest in poetry which has already been translated. After studying the Persian masters he tells us that he turned

his attention to the critical examination of the Turkish poets,
all of whom, starting with their protagonist the Chaghatáy
Mír ʿAlí Shír, he found to be imitators of the Íránians.
Next we have a few remarks on the injury done to Turkish
poetry by those early writers having substituted the Perso-
Arabian prosodic system for the native 'finger-counting' or
syllabic metres, and on the relations thus established between
the poetry of the Ottomans and that of the Persians and
Arabs. Ziyá then mentions his great desire to be a poet,
and states that though his studies may not have enabled
him to attain this honour, they have at least given him a
critical knowledge of the art. He is now past his forty-fourth
year, [1] and reflecting on the transitoriness of life, he is filled
with longing to leave behind him some memorial which will
preserve his name from oblivion, when he bethinks him of
the story of Qitmír the dog of the Seven Sleepers of Ephesus, [2]
and how his name, though he was only a beast, has been
handed with theirs down the ages by reason of his faithful
service to these noble men. Ziyá will therefore follow his
example, and do a service to the illustrious poets. When
during the course of his reading he came across any verses
which specially pleased him, it had been his custom to copy
them into an album. He now set to work to arrange this
collection as an ordered anthology. He has preserved, he
says, the old spelling; while as Chaghatáy is, so to speak,
the 'mother' of Ottoman Turkish, he has felt bound to grant
it a place. He has passed the poets in review, and criticised
each according to the best of his judgment. He has also
included the best-known works of his contemporaries. He

---

[1] This would give 1289 or 1290 as the date of the preface to the Kharábát,
allowing Ziyá to have been born in 1245.

[2] The Seven Sleepers of Ephesus are reckoned as saints by the Muslims;
they and their dog Qitmír are mentioned in Súra xviii of the Koran.

has inserted in his collection all his favourite pieces; yet in order to show both merits and faults, he has given examples of every style. He then bids the reader think how many books he must have read and how much labour the compilation must have cost him. This section of the preface winds up thus: 'Since the topers[1] meet therein, I have named this book the 'Tavern'; none would have given credit had I entitled it the 'Mosque', as not many poets frequent that place.'

In the next section, 'Concerning the Conditions of Poetry in Turkey,' the author gives a brief account of the development of Ottoman poetry as he understood it. He ignores all the archaic writers and begins with Ahmed Pasha, Nejátí and Zátí, who, he says, laid the foundations of Turkish literature. Although the matter of these early poets is good, their language is uncouth, and owing to the changes that have taken place, their idiom is only with difficulty intellegible nowadays. The advancement of the language was much assisted by the encouragement which Sultans Selím I and Suleymán I gave to the poets, notably to Báqí, who, although obsolete words still occur in his verses, may justly be entitled the first reformer of the language. After his time the literary idiom became more thoroughly Persianised, chiefly through the influence of Nef'í and Nábí, the result being that it grew to be the most copious in the world.[3] Sábit and Sámí, however, introduced a number of prosodial solecisms, which, being adopted by Rághib and ʿAsim, became the rule for subsequent poets.

The section which follows deals with the necessary quali-

---

[1] The old poets were fond of speaking of themselves as 'topers.'

[2] احوال اشعار روم.

[3] Perhaps this is true; during the seventeenth century, at any rate, every word in the Persian and Arabic dictionaries was a possible Ottoman word.

fications of the Poet.[1] Two things are needful before a man
can be a poet, of which the first is natural genius, the
second culture. The first is the gift of God, for unless a
man is born a poet, he can never become one: yet native
talent, however great, is insufficient without diligent study
and application. The typical poet is described as a man of
free and easy temper, fond of pleasure, not over scrupulous
in his religious duties, nor (except in his verses) particularly
subservient to the great. He ought, we are told, to be neither
rich nor poor. The reader is counselled to throw aside prejudice
and learn the languages of Europe, as one cannot otherwise
become a perfect poet. For in the poetry of these languages
there is another eloquence, by which 'the mirror of thy
heart will be polished and the strength of thy soul doubled.'
At the same time one must not copy this to the extent of
losing one's own nationality; East and West are essentially
different, and it is not good to destroy one's individuality.
The poets of the West worship 'the Muses', and write very
artistic dramas. These, especially when played by good actors,
are very powerful; but it is a mistake to imagine that they
are all lessons in morals, for though one in a hundred may be so,
with the remaining ninety and nine it is otherwise. Poetry,
continues Ziyá, is the flower of speech; and it is because
royal edicts have not always sounded sweet that kings have
been wont to regard poets with favour.[2] It is, moreover, by the
words of poets that the names of monarchs are saved from
oblivion: who would ever mention the Atabek[3] but for Saʿdí?
It is Jámí and Newáʾí who have preserved the fame of

[1] مشروط و احوال شاعرى.

[2] That the poets by praising the kings in their verses may gain for these
rulers the admiration of the people.

[3] The Atábek Abú Bakr ibn Saʿd ibn Zangí, the prince of Shíráz to whom
Saʿdí dedicated his immortal Gulistán.

Huseyn Bayqará. The words of true poetry are eternal; the shifts and changes of time cannot destroy them. Whosoever can utter such words is an emperor in the realms of culture; his díwán will abide till the end of time; and while his enemies will pass away and be forgotten, his name and fame will endure for ever, — and in this lies his revenge.

In the succeeding section, 'On the Characteristics of the Ottoman Poets,'[1] Ziyá passes in review a considerable number of the more important of his predecessors, devoting a few lines to the criticism of each in turn. As almost all these criticisms have already been discussed when dealing with the several poets to whom they refer, it is unnecessary in this place to do more than remark that it is hard to imagine by what principle Ziyá was guided when deciding whom to mention. The critical remarks are prefaced by a few lines in which we are told that those who have studied the subject divide Turkish poetry into three periods: the Early, which ends with Báqí (beginning presumably with Ahmed, Nejátí and Zátí, whom a previous section describes as having laid the foundations); the Middle, which goes down to Nábí; and the Later, extending to the writer's own time. We are further informed that during the first and second of these periods poetry suffered no deterioration; but that during the third, poets have become rare.

This section is followed by two others similar in character, but of less extent, dealing respectively with the Persian and Arabian poets.

The preface to the Kharábát is brought to a conclusion by an epilogue in which Ziyá, after saying that his collection does, as it were, prefigure the Judgment Day, the poets of many lands and ages being gathered together to receive

---

1. احوال شعرای روم.

sentence according to their works, offers his anthology as a guide to aspirant poets and as a souvenir to the 'men of heart.' He then seeks to disarm adverse criticism by reminding the would-be caviller that poems which appear trivial to him may be dear to others, that the world is not confined to him alone, and that a single couplet which appeals to a man, or which meets his case, is of more value to him than a whole díwán. Again, the present collection is but a compendium, it does not profess to contain everything that is good; 'I plunged into an ocean full of jewels, I took just as many as I was able, the sea is still brimful.' And last of all the compiler claims indulgence on the score of his failing health. 'When the body no longer enjoys health the mind cannot remain unaffected; when I made this book my body was racked with pain and my heart was full of anguish; all my days have passed in troubles, and suffering has been the fruit that I have gathered; I have written as I could, well or ill; is not the plight of the sick man known? I trust, therefore, that the courteous and refined will hold my excuse worthy of acceptance.'

These excuses and entreaties of Ziyá availed but little with the most illustrious of his whilom colleagues. The first volume of the Kharábát was published in Sha'bán 1291 (Sept.—Oct. 1874); before the year was out Kemál Bey had penned and sent to the compiler, from Famagusta in Cyprus, where he was then involuntarily residing as nominal governor, an attack upon the book, which for bitterness of tone is scarcely inferior to the Zafer-Náme itself. Ziyá had indeed laid himself open to criticism; he was not much of a critic — nothing where Kemál came; — and his selection of poems is no doubt a long way from being the best that could be made; his preface, moreover, is crude and ill-digested, often inconsequent, sometimes self-contradictory; but all this is insufficient to account 'for the acrimony of the attack. The real motive of this violent onslaught of Kemál was threefold. In the first place, he held — and held rightly — that at this time of day a man of learning and a professed reformer like Ziyá had no business to set up as models of literary excellence many of the pieces included in the Kharábát. In the second place, the critic, ever a sturdy defender of the national cause, was disgusted at the sycophantic poems which, since his return from Europe, Ziyá had been in the habit of addressing to Sultan ʿAbd-ul-ʿAzíz, and of which several are printed in his collection. In the third place, Kemál felt it as a personal slight that, whilst all the other contemporary poets — including the compiler himself — were largely quoted, he was represented only by three rather feeble juvenile couplets, although he had, as Ziyá knew perfectly well, written a great number of poems, many of which were of high merit. Whatever may have been the reason for this shabby treatment of an old fellow-worker, whether Ziyá was jealous of his friend's greater poetic gift, or whether, as is more likely, he dreaded offending the Palace by quoting one who was anything but a persona grata, certain it is that Kemál took the matter to heart, and did not hesitate to avail himself of the opportunity which a criticism of the book offered to take revenge for what was to him an unmerited personal affront.

Under such circumstances strict fairness is not to be looked for; none the less, along with much that is beside the mark, being obviously written with the deliberate intention to wound, there is in this review a great deal of pure literary criticism which is extremely valuable and suggestive. The literary instinct in Kemál was too true and too strong to permit of his writing anything that had not in some degree a real and enduring value; and while we cannot but think it would

have been better for the author's fair fame had he magna-
nimously ignored an old ally's discourtesy, it is neverthe-
less true that had this review not been written, Turkish
literature would have been the poorer by one of its best
and most remarkable essays in criticism.

On the appearance of the second volume in the following
year, Kemál wrote on it another similar review.

I have been assured by Turks who were personally
acquainted with both Kemál Bey and Ziyá Pasha that notwithstanding the unpleasantness of this incident the two
poets remained good friends down to the death of the latter.
So long as Ziyá lived these letters remained unpublished,
but in 1298 (1881), a year or so after his death, they were
printed in Ebu-z-Ziyá's Magazine, the first under the title
of Takhríb-i Kharábát 'The Demolition of the Tavern,' the
second under that of Ta῾qíb 'The Pursuit.' [1]

In spite of all the strictures of Kemál Bey, the Kharábát
is an extremely useful book. It is unquestionably the best
anthology of old Turkish poetry in existence; and in its
three volumes it presents a fairly adequate picture of the
achievements of the Asiatic School. No doubt every reader
thinks with Kemál that he could improve the selection by
omitting this and inserting that; but such is the common
lot of all anthologies. A graver drawback is the evident
haste and lack of care with which the preface was written;
this, which has led to several inconsistencies, seriously impairs
the value of a piece of work which, for all its faults, is yet

---

[1] The Takhríb runs through six consecutive numbers of the Mejmú῾a-i
Ebu-z-Ziyá, beginning with No. 19 in the Second Volume, the issue for 15
Jemazi-ul-Akhir 1298. The Ta῾qíb begins in No. 30 in the Third Volume —
that for 15 Rebí῾-ul-Evvel 1300 — and runs on to No. 36. Both articles
were afterwards (in 1303) published separately by Ebu-z-Ziyá Tevfíq Bey
among the volumes of his 'Library' (Kutub-Kháne-i Ebu-z-Ziyá).

full of interest. But here the state of the author's health may be pleaded in extenuation.

Less easy to forgive is the egotism which has led the compiler to insert among his selections page after page from his own díwán, and that to so disproportionate an extent that he holds a position of exceptional prominence in a collection where the canons of taste should have ruled precisely the reverse. It might perhaps be urged in excuse that, no edition of his poems having at that time been published, the author was naturally anxious to ensure for his favourite verses such immortality as he could. But here his case was in no wise different from that of many — probably of most — of his contemporaries, including Kemál Bey himself. From the beginning it had always been the exception, rather than the rule, for a Turkish poet to collect his own díwán, or even to see it collected during his lifetime. It was much more usual to defer the collecting and arranging of a poet's works until after his death, when the task generally devolved upon some enthusiastic disciple or admiring friend, — of which practice we have seen many examples in the course of this History.

Brave and earnest, talented and industrious, Ziyá rendered signal and enduring service alike to the cause of progress and to the new learning. But he was lacking in stamina; if he did not fall, he at least grew faint in the heat of battle. The years of exile wrecked his health and broke his spirit. Poor Ziyá, he had overestimated the strength that was in him! Yet but for him, the literary revolution had not been the swift success it was; while had he only been the leader, it would have died, a mere flash in the pan.

Ziyá's famous Terjí'-Bend consists of twelve stanzas, ten of which are here translated; the remaining two are omitted as they are somewhat commonplace and tend to detract from the effect of the poem. The refrain is an ancient Arabic couplet here used by the poet as a sort of commentary on his own reflections, in fearful submission, in bewildered consternation, or in bitter irony, — as the reader will. Since Ziyá's employment of it, this distich has become a household word among the Turks.

Terjíʿ-Bend [468].

How passing strange a school this workshop of creation shows!
Its every fabric doth some script of the unknown expose.
The whirling heaven is a mill whose yield is agony;
Bewildered man is e'en the grain it grinds the while it goes. [1]
Like to a demon fierce and fell its offspring it devours:
How strange a nest doth this old hostelry of earth disclose!
If one should heedful scan the shows of all existent things,
Behold a dream, a phantasy, a tale of joys and woes.
All things soever in the world are borne towards an end;
Spring into autumn glides, and summer's heat to winter's snows.
Belike 'tis man will never win Eternal Truth unto;
All faiths and creeds appear to reason vague and futile shows.
O wherefore, Lord, is all this bitter stress and strife of pain,
The while a crust of bread is all the need man really knows?
There is no buckler underneath yon dome of turquoise hue; [2]
Each atom is the butt 'gainst which fierce Fate his arrows throws.
The scheme of the Everlasting Will is working out its end;
But means are all the seeming good and ill that e'er arose.
All things existent are the workings of some mighty Power;
No circlings of the Heaven's wheel, no tricks of Fortune, those.
    'Glory to Him before whose work all intellect is dazed!
    'Glory to Him before whose might the wisest stand amazed!'

With spheres beyond all reckoning the boundless sky is dight,
Compared to which this earth were scarce an atom in our sight.

---

[1] As Tevfíq Bey points out, the figure in this couplet recalls the incident with his lala which first directed the author's childish thoughts to poetry.
[2] The sky.

A thousand blazing suns are there, a myriad shining moons,
A hundred thousand stars, and many a wandering planet bright.
Each sun with its own satellites is journeying on its road,
Whilst other satellites in turn attend each satellite.
Each sun a special virtue o'er its own dependents sheds,
While ever hidden from its feres is each dependent's plight.
Around its centre every system ceaselessly revolves,
In its own orbit every sphere Eternal Grace doth sight.
Myriad existences are scattered through each system vast,
In every spacious sphere a thousand worlds [1] are brought to light.
Each several being for a thousand beings is the source;
Each several world suggests a myriad other worlds forthright.
In every atom lies a virtue special to itself,
In every frame according to its nature is the spright.
The changing seasons and the years are different in each world;
Nay, every land a different reckoning of time doth cite.
In brief, this boundless ocean is an ocean that doth lead
On every side into the dizzy whirlpool of affright.
   'Glory to Him before whose work all intellect is dazed!
   'Glory to Him before whose might the wisest stand amazed!'

This mighty mote of earth's a mote on such wise fashionéd
That separate therefrom not any mote may fix its stead.
A fiery ball it is whose heart is scorching lambent flame,
Whose crust is scarred with many a river-course and ocean-bed.
Its crust, if thou compare it with that heart of raging fire,
Is even as the vines that over dome or cupole spread.
This crust it is that night and day for every living thing
Provideth all that needful is and yieldeth daily bread.
What time the fiery subterranean dragon breatheth forth,
The burning mountains, showering flame, make earth to quake for dread.
Even as by a shade of glass a lamp is circled round,
By limpid air this giant mote is all encomppasséd.
From off that world-embracing board it is that every day
All creatures that have breath, whate'er their rank or power, are fed.
This dot it is that marketh off the left hand from the right;

---

[1] By 'worlds' is meant 'Kingdoms' of natural objects, such as plants, animals and so on.

From hence the intellect sets out where'er its flight is sped.
Here each existent atom tasteth life's hilarity,
Here each created thing must drain the draught that dooms it dead.
All creatures lie, reposing calm upon the couch of ease,
Upon a burning globe they sleep sans fear, sans thought, sans dread.
　'Glory to Him before whose work all intellect is dazed!
　'Glory to Him before whose might the wisest stand amazed!'

The lion's cruel fangs do rend the screaming fawn, their prey;
The fierce and ravening wolf devours the sheep, ah! welaway!
The fly, though guiltless, yet becomes the hungry spider's meal;
E'en so the royal falcon doth the harmless pigeon slay;
The tortoise all defenceless must the eagle's victim fall;
And with the helpless frog the snake his hunger doth allay;
The chicken, though he doth no wrong, is mangled by the kite;
The mouse, although he sins not, by the cat is torn in tway;
The bitter eager hawk likewise the hapless sparrow kills;
The buzzard's cruel talons too the blameless pheasant flay;
The bird, though swift of wing, becomes the grovelling serpent's meal;
The fish that swims the sea becomes the fowl of heaven's prey;
'Tis greed of pearls that handeth o'er the diver to the shark;
'Tis lust of grain that doth the partridge to the snare betray;
'Tis for the pearl anear its heart the oyster riven is;
'Tis for its song the nightingale imprisoned pines away;
His castor 'tis that brings about the luckless beaver's doom;
His fur it is that doth the sable unto death bewray.
The universal law is this: — The strong shall slay the weak.
On earth, in air, in sea this hideous carnage rageth aye.
　'Glory to Him before whose work all intellect is dazed!
　'Glory to Him before whose might the wisest stand amazed!'

At times the sun, at times a star, yea, e'en at times a stone
Hath been the trusted god fore which a race has fallen prone.
Now to the calf,[1] and now to fire, Ormuzd and Ahriman,[2]
And now to darkness, now to light, have worship's rites been shown.

---

[1] Referring to the worship of the golden calf by the Jews.
[2] Ormuzd and Ahriman, the Principles of Good and Evil with the Zoroastrians.

7

Of old time beauty, wisdom, love were all as gods revered; [1]
For many a year in every land were idols served alone.
At length the season came wherein God's Unity was learned,
But e'en through that a thousand strifes, disputes and feuds were sown.
The mind now thought Creator and Created one, now two,
Believed now endless difference, now final union.
Some held the Substance manifold, the Attributes as one,
Then in one Origin did many an origin depone.
Each one desires to shape a God conformable unto
Those thoughts and aspirations which in truth are all his own.
As different as mind and matter each from other is,
So different the varied faiths and creeds the world hath known.
How passing strange that every folk holds others' creeds in scorn,
And deems the way of righteousness belongs to it alone,
While yet with all this difference the aim of every sect
Is but with true devotion one Creator's rule to own!

   'Glory to Him before whose work all intellect is dazed!
   'Glory to Him before whose might the wisest stand amazed!'

The roses smile, the nightingale breathes out his life in sighs,
His fee is all the leech's thought the while the sick man dies.
The corpse of him who riches had is e'en as carrion,
Like vultures are the lavers and the heirs with greedy eyes.
Upon the couch of luxury the city lord reclines,
The stranger starves within the dust of scorn in woful guise.
The smiling taper sheddeth radiance o'er the joyous feast,
Amidst its flame, with crippled wing, the moth unheeded dies.
Garlic and onion freely smile like tulip or narcisse,
While prisoned close in narrow vial sweetest perfume lies.
The sordid fool reposeth glad on cushions of delight,
While in the stoke-hole of contempt croucheth the good and wise.
Earthly prosperity is oft the lot of ignorance,
What time the world a crust for wisdom's evening-meal denies.
The banquet of society receives the false and vile,
The spirit of the world doth oft the true and leal despise.
The gifted poet many a time becomes the jest of fools,

---

[1] As by the ancient Greeks.

The wise and learned many a time the idiot's mirth supplies.
The feeble and opprest must often want for daily bread
What while a cruel tyrant's deeds to fame and glory rise.
　'Glory to Him before whose work all intellect is dazed!
　'Glory to Him before whose might the wisest stand amazed!'

O Lord, how comes it every man of learning here below
Must through the curse of knowledge ever rest and peace forego?
O Lord, why is it that with every wise man here on earth
The measure of his gifts is still the measure of his woe?
His peace of mind is gone, whatever side he turn his glance;
His understanding is abased, where'er his thoughts may go.
With knowledge as the only weight for understanding's scales
Is't possible the utmost truth of things to weigh and know?
Thus impotent may any vision ever win to see
The final verity of all the things and haps that show?
And then, as though the burden of this sorrow were too light,
From fools' o'erbearing tyranny in blood his vitals flow.
I know not; is it ordered in the canon of the world
That ever upon earth the brutish folk shall prosper so?
Since e'er the world hath been the world this rule hath still prevailed,
Before the vilest lout the man of heart is humbled low.
The dullard prosperous and courted lifts on high his head
Contemned and destitute the sage must ever humbly bow.
Fair Fortune doth caress the fool, crowning his every hope,
While fickle Fate the wise and good to beggary doth throw. [1]
　'Glory to Him before whose work all intellect is dazed!
　'Glory to Him before whose might the wisest stand amazed!'

The Father of Mankind was cast from Eden's happy plain;
As place of trial for Abraham his offspring's neck was ta'en;
The dole of separation from his son made Jacob weep;
The saintly Joseph's biding-place was e'en the well of bane;
Ailments and aches of frame and limb made Job to groan full sore;

---

[1] These five last couplets have a peculiar appropriateness in the East, where not unfrequently those in authority are both ignorant and overbearing.

And Zacharias to the saw must needs his head constrain; [1]
John the Apostle [2] was beheaded by fell tyranny;
Jesus the Fatherless endured full much of grief and pain;
At Tá'if were the Prophet's shoon to ruby turned, [3] and then
Yon lustrous pearls were on the Day of Uhud broke atwain; [4]
For hunger's pangs he bound the stone fast to his blessed waist, [5]
Full little recked the Lord of Humankind of wordly gain; [6]
Poisoned, from hence unto the Other World set forth the Leal; [7]

[1] According to the Muhammedan legend, Herod, when he had determined to slay John, was fearful lest some evil should overtake him through the prayers of his victim's father the saintly Zacharias. He therefore determined to murder the old man before slaying his son. Zacharias, becoming aware of this purpose, fled, and while on his way, saw a tree the trunk of which was split open as if to offer him a hiding-place. He concealed himself therein, whereon the trunk closed upon him, but a corner of his robe remained hanging out. Herod's emissaries passing by met an old man who, having enquired their errand, told them that he whom they sought was concealed in the tree, showing them the corner of the robe that was hanging out. At the instigation of this old man — who was Satan in disguise — they got a great saw and cut longwise down through the trunk of the tree, so that the saint was cloven in two from the crown downwards.

[2] John the Baptist is referred to.

[3] At Tá'if the Prophet Muhammed was stoned by some heathen and wounded in the legs, so that they were stained with the blood which ran down over his feet.

[4] At Uhud the Prophet was struck on the mouth by a stone thrown by Ibn-Abi-Waqqás, and two of his front teeth were broken.

[5] Referring to the hardships the Prophet underwent during his wanderings. In a former note (vol. iii, p. 56, n. 1) the custom of tying a stone against the stomach to repel hunger has been already spoken of. The poet Sámí hints at this practice in the following rather pretty little conceit on a qibla-náme (for qibla-numá), as the Turks call a particular kind of compass arranged to point out the direction of Mekka; the compass itself is here likened to a pilgrim-lover seeking with fear and trembling the dwelling of his loved one, the needle being his staff; and the china face on which the directions are marked, his 'contentment stone.'

باغرنه طاش باصوب آلمش النه آهن عصا کوی جانانی ارار دنریعرك قبله نما

'Stone against its middle bounden, and with iron staff in hand,
'Trembling sore, the compass ever seeketh out the Loved One's land.'

There is also a proverb, آجلقدن کوبکنه طاش باغلدی 'for hunger he has bound the stone against his navel.

[6] Referring to the Prophet's simple life.

[7] Es-Siddíq 'the Leal' was the title bestowed by the Prophet on his father-

And by the sword of doom at last was martyred ʿOmar slain; [1]
And martyrdom befell him too who ordered the Koran; [2]
The Blessed Hayder sank at last beneath the blade profane; [3]
And Hasan, poisoned, passed away to Paradise above; [4]
And foully murdered was the Monarch of the martyr-train. [5]
In whomsoe'er the love of the Divine doth master all,
To him in that same fashion woe and anguish still pertain.
  'Glory to Him before whose work all intellect is dazed!
  'Glory to Him before whose might the wisest stand amazed!'

Who made the human race this woful impotence to bear?
Who raised that race on high above all worlds exalted fair?
Who makes the devil and the flesh the instruments of sin?
Who casteth into hell all those that lust doth overbear?
Who drove Mansúr into the region of 'I am the Truth'?
Who gave the Holy Law the right to slay him then and there? [6]
Who made the wine unlawful and of bitter taste the while?
Who taught Jemshíd the bowl and heady potion to prepare? [7]
Who made the Jew deny the miracles of Heavenly Truth?
Who breathéd the Messiah into Mary debonair?

---

in-law Ebú Bekr, who became his immediate successor in the government of
the Faithful. According to one tradition, he died of the effects of poison
administered a year before by some Jews.

[1] ʿOmar, Ebú Bekr's successor, was assassinated by a Persian slave.

[2] ʿOsmán (in Arabic, ʿUthmán,) was the Prophet's son-in-law and ʿOmar's
successor. He was murdered by a band of conspirators in his eighty-second
year. It was he who made the final revision of the Koran.

[3] Hayder, more often called ʿAlí, another son-in-law of the Prophet, and
ʿOsmán's successor, was killed with a poisoned sword by Ibn Muljem. Ebu
Bekr, ʿOmar, ʿOsmán and ʿAlí, the first four Caliphs, are collectively called
the Khulefá-yi Ráshidín or 'Right-guided Caliphs.'

[4] Hasan, the son of ʿAlí, was poisoned in Medína by his wife Jaʿda at
the instigation of Muʿáwiya, the usurping Caliph and founder of the Umayyad,
dynasty who had promised to marry her to his son Yezíd.

[5] That is Huseyn, ʿAlí's other son, and the chief of the martyrs of Kerbelá.

[6] Mansúr, (properly Huseyn ibn Mansúr, called el-Halláj, the Wool-carder)
the oft-mentioned martyr of the mystics, put to death by the decree of the
ʿulemá, the official interpreters of the Holy Law.

[7] Jemshíd, one of the ancient legendary Persian Kings, who is reputed
to have discovered the art of making wine.

Who gave Sufyán [1] and Ja'da, [2] Ibn Muljem, [3] aye, and Shimr [4]
The hardihood the foulest of all infamies to dare?
Who 'sent Nasír-ud-Dín of Tús to counsel Hulágú?
Who caused Musta'sim all his trust with Ibn 'Alqam to share? [5]
Who makes the sick man stand in need of physic and of drug?
Who makes the balm remedial its healing virtue wear?
From whom is it the bee hath learned the geometric art?
Who is it that hath taught the nightingale his plaintive air?
Who is it round this Work-shop draws the veil of mystery?
Who is it that inspireth man to search this everywhere?
　'Glory to Him before whose work all intellect is dazed!
　'Glory to Him before whose might the wisest stand amazed!'

＊　＊　＊　＊　＊　＊　＊　＊　＊　＊　＊　＊

He changeth morn to even and He turneth night to day;
He maketh summer winter and He maketh autumn May.
From the death-throe He bringeth life, He makes the dead to live;
He turns the clay to man, He turns the body back to clay.
For Abraham His might transformed the Fire into the Light; [6]
To Moses did His wisdom high the Light as Fire display. [7]

---

[1] Ebu Sufyán, though he eventually embraced Islám, was for long among the most determined of the Prophet's opponents.

[2] Ja'da, Hasan's treacherous wife and murderess.

[3] Ibn Muljem, the murderer of 'Alí.

[4] Shimr, a commander in Yezíd's army which defeated Huseyn at Kerbelá, and the reputed slayer of the martyr Ímám.

[5] Nasír-ud-Dín of Tús, a very famous philosopher and astronomer, was attached to the service of Hulágú the Mongol conqueror, whom he urged to march against Baghdád. Ibn 'Alqam (properly Ibnu'l-'Alqamí), the treacherous vezír of el-Musta'sim billáh, the last Caliph of the house of 'Abbás, was the means of admitting into Baghdád the Mongols, who thereupon murdered the Caliph, massacred the people, and laid the city in ruins. All these historical allusions are of course familiar to every educated Muslim.

[6] Referring to the legend according to which Nimrod cast Abraham into a huge blazing furnace for blaspheming his divinity, whereupon God sent the Angel Gabriel who changed for Abraham the fire into a garden of flowers. The story is practically the same as that of Shadrach, Meshach and Abednego in the Book of Daniel.

[7] In the Burning Bush. With the mystics the terms Fire and Light are used to typify respectively the Awfulness and the Beauty of the Divinity.

Showing the Leylá-beauty Shírín-sweet before his eyes,
For dole of love He made Ferhád Mejún-distracted stray.
He makes a heart bereft of peace for long through some desire;
For some fond hope He makes a soul for years to thole dismay.
He overthrows a kingdom for some greedy tyrant's sake;
He casts through some intriguer a whole nation in deray.
He fosters in all luxury a body many a year,
And then at last He yields it to the clutch of death as prey.
He maketh one a treasure-hoard of knowledge year on year,
And in the dust sepulchral at the end He doth him lay.
Ziyá, the sage is he who doth his helplessness confess,
And taketh warning by the things that pass before him aye.
Throughout His Kingdom ever rules the Truth 'e'en as He will':
The universe, e'en as He please, He makes or doth away.
  'Glory to Him before whose work all intellect is dazed!
  'Glory to Him before whose might the wisest stand amazed!'

The following little ballad was written by Ziyá in imitation of the Turkís or folk-songs; the curious inconsequence, the lack of apparent connection between the lines even of a single stanza, is characteristic of the type.

Turkí [469].

The sun is sinking, and the evening-dusk is falling now,
And from the vale the shepherd-lad is piping soft and low.
May He who made thee keep the safe, for very young art thou.
  Come, join the flock, my little lamb, the wolf might seize on thee:
  Parted at last from thy dear love, my little one, thou'lt be.

Since that the Lord hath made of me thy slave for aye and aye,
Where'er thou treadest it were meet my face and eyes I lay.
Be not deceived by rivals' craft, but heed the words I say.
  Come, join the flock, my little lamb, the wolf might seize on thee:
  Parted at last from thy dear love, my little one, thou'lt be.

The mist wraps all the mountain round, the rival can't be seen;
One may not win unto one's love, the hunter 's laid his gin.

Wine is not drunk in company of faithless friend, I ween.
Come, join the flock, my little lamb, the wolf might seize on thee :
Parted at last from thy dear love, my little one, thou'lt be.

Of the sixty-six stanzas of the Zafer-Náme I have translated thirty-three. These thirty-three have been selected as being either characteristic or interesting; and, taken as a whole, they give a fairly adequate idea of the poem.

From the Zafer-Náme [470].

Lo! what a royal triumph! glorious! splendid! of high degree!
Lo! what a joyous conquest! lo! what a banner of victory!
'Twere meet that Zál and Rustem [1] cry in Heaven, as they wondering see : —
'God bless us all! what a meteor bright of loftiest radiancy!
'God save us all! what a wondrous triumph crowned by Fortune free!'

Here is the history of the past, if of argument there's need; [2]
The fights that have been fought on earth are many and many indeed;
But thus say men below, with angels bright above agreed : —
'The truth is this, that never since the spheres began to speed
'Hath any ever won so brave a victory to see!'

In dread looked the earth to the sky, the sky looked to earth in dismay;
And each in its terror sought some place where to hide away ;
The peoples of earth and sky wailed and cried in dire affray;
The welkin shook with the shouts : 'God grant him to live for aye!'
And quaked the earth with the cries : 'Exalted on high be he!'

Let us search all records through since history hath begun,
E'en from the furthest East to where sinks the westering sun.
Heroes and conquerors bold have arisen — many an one, —
But ne'er to a triumph grand like to this hath any won,
Iskender nor Hulágú, Hannibal nor Cæsar, nay!

[1] Zál and Rustem, the legendary Persian heroes.
[2] I. e. If the greatness of ʿAlí Pasha's victory over the Cretan rebels be questioned, we appeal to history to show a more brilliant triumph.

Waving on Candia's towers, his flag triumphant flew;
And the charm of the words he wrote [1] did Europe's heart subdue.
To save the State in sooth was all that he held in view;
The might of his sword and pen hath conquered Crete anew
    Although that its folk were bent on independency.

'If the aim and purpose be but to rule the State aright,
'Such number of lands and towns will all endeavour blight.'
Himself did invent that rule illumed with wisdom's light. [2]
He freed the State in sooth from a passing parlous plight;
    Elsewise were affairs to-day in a sad perplexity.

[1] ʿAlí Pasha's official notes promising reforms, etc.

[2] ʿAlí Pasha maintained, not without some truth, that much of the difficulty of governing the Ottoman Empire arose from the number and diversity of its subject races; and in order to remove, or at least alleviate, this difficulty he was in favour of granting a species of home-rule to certain districts where one or other of those subject races was in a large numerical preponderance. This was a scheme for which much might have been said, but it was hardly likely to commend itself to a Turkish patriot zealous of maintaining the supremacy of his people. In the following passage from the Commentary the idea and its originator are both turned into ridicule by Ziyá who here for the first (but by no means the last) time makes Husní Pasha's fictitious work an instrument for the expression of his own political views: 'In the perspicacious opinion of our lord ʿAlí Pasha the absence of good administration throughout the Sublime Empire is due solely to the extent of its territories and to the want of cohesion amongst these. Thus if a number of districts were cut off and formed into compact governments, like the Kingdom of Greece, the administration would in the future certainly be improved. Now this sagacious suggestion is of the inventions of that Fountain-head of Perfections, and none before him ever uttered it. And by this sage scheme it is that Crete has been placed under a special government, and the Empire relieved from that trouble. Although such diversities and the symptoms of bad administration may still be seen in the Principalities (Walachia and Moldavia), in Servia, in Montenegro, in Egypt, in Arabia and in Bulgaria, it is beyond doubt that, through the lofty zeal of His Highness, these troubles also will shortly be removed from the Empire.

"What sorrow for the nation's bulwarks buttressed by thy like?" '
This Persian hemistich which Ziyá makes Husní quote may be read either as a question or as an exclamation.

چہ غم دیوارِ اُمّتِرا کہ باشد چون تو پشتیبان

While safe and snug was his home in the midst of his maidens fair,
And while with his servants' jests his nights enlivened were,[1]
Unbidden did he all such delight and peace forswear;
He chose this hard campaign in the winter-tide to share,[2]
  While never an one had wished of him to be rid or free.

There were vessels twenty-and-five his high commands to obey;
He took one Greekish steamer, the fruit of a year's essay.[3]
Although he ne'er had studied things naval till that day,
He wrought that on the squadron nor slight nor stigma lay;
  Full worthy he an admiral of the English fleet to be.[4]

When forth to that bitter war did this valiant champion go,
The very thought of his sword made the paynim hordes bow low.

[1] Ziyá here takes the opportunity to deal a blow at some of his opponents, notably at his old patron Mustafá Fázil Pasha who had played him false. Husní is made to say in his Commentary: 'That is, his servants such as Vehbí Mollá, Sá'ib Bey, Billúrí Mehemmed Efendi, ʿOmer Fá'iz Efendi, Khalíl Bey and Mustafá Fázil Pasha, whose nights are usually spent in drinking and making merry at the private feasts of His Highness our benefactor, and who, when their pates get heated, amuse His Highness with ribaldries of which larrikins would be ashamed.'

[2] ʿAlí Pasha arrived in Crete on the 28th of September 1867.

[3] The Greek steamer Arkadi, after having repeatedly run the blockade bearing arms for the rebels and landing filibusters, was taken by the Imperial vessel ʿIzz-ud-Dín.

[4] The 'Summary of the Meaning' which winds up the commentary on this stanza is a good example of Ziyá's satirical praise. 'When he who is versed in all learning and science, to wit, His Highness the accomplished ʿAlí Pasha, set in motion the wheel of departure to conquer and restore Crete, that island was blockaded by twenty-five government vessels. Notwithstanding this, the steamer Arkadi and Russian and Italian steamers were puffing about bearing stores to the island rebels. At length, after a year's untold efforts, he succeeded in capturing the aforesaid. steamer, and by this marvellous victory he saved the honour of the fleet from any hurt. Now when one who never in all his life had seen any sea except the Bosphorus or any ship beyond a row-boat is able to achieve so glorious a triumph solely through his own energy and ability, is he not worthy to be an admiral in the English navy? For the English naval chiefs are more skilful than those of any other nation; but while they have to study a long time in their schools and do not become admirals until after forty or fifty years, our benefactor has attained to this degree of perfection through his inborn genius or through the sheer grace of God. O happy Empire!'

He held the soldiers back, nor let one pursue the foe; [1]
How 'Pardon is the alms of victory' he did show, [2]
Nor swept from the face of earth the dastard rebel crew.

His skill in all arts that be unto everyone is known;
But in letters more than all is his wondrous talent shown.
E'en supposing we could not prove these pretensions one by one, [3]
That Note [4] of his which recounts all the deeds that he hath done
Unmatched and unrivalled stands for its rhetoric's brilliancy.

No eye may pierce to his reed with art invested fair,
For circling o'er its head doth the halo of wisdom flare.

[1] In the Commentary on this line Ziyá says through his monthpiece Husní Pasha: 'When that Mine of Magnanimity (i. e. ꜤAlí Pasha) was in Crete, the Greek rebels used often to attack the guard-houses held by the Muslim troops and to seize captives whom they murdered with all kinds of tortures, and to come down into the environs of the towns and destroy the vineyards and orchards. In brief, there is not a brutality that they have left undone; still His Highness forbade the troops to pursue them. It was even as in the Montenegrin trouble, when, though the mountaineers used to cut off the noses and ears of the Muslim soldiers, our lord ꜤAlí Pasha would permit no attack on them, in order that the question might be settled by diplomacy.'

Of course, ꜤAlí Pasha's abstention from chastising those malefactors as they deserved was really brought about by the pressure put upon the Porte by certain of the European embassies. Ziyá knew this perfectly well, and his reflections on the Vezir's conduct in this and some other similar cases are unfair. None the less an Ottoman minister who seems to yield over much to foreign insolence can hardly expect to stand well with his countrymen, who naturally and justly can see no reason why they should not deal with their revolted subjects in the same way as Englishmen have dealt with revolted Indians, Frenchmen with revolted Algerians, and Russians with revolted Poles and Turcomans.

[2] اَلْعَفْوُ زَكاة اَلظَّفَرِ 'Pardon is the alms of Victory', is a hadís.

[3] These pretensions, i. e. our claim that he is skilled in all the arts that be.

[4] The Note which ꜤAlí Pasha presented to the Sultan on his return from Crete. In it he gave an account of all he had done in the island and of the measures he had taken to ensure tranquility. It was published in the Constantinople newspapers. Having satirised ꜤAlí's exploits in Crete, Ziyá now proceeds to turn his literary and other accomplishments into ridicule. ꜤAlí Pasha was not, and did not pretend to be, a man of letters; there is, however, a ghazel by him (the only one known) in Fatín's Tezkiré.

This verse from his Victory-Book [1] read thou with heed and care:
In questions and upon points that touch the loved one's hair [2]
The threads suggestive coil at his pen's foot verily.

Whatever thing he writes, the world is compelled to praise;
Whatever thing he doth, the people admire always.
How could it be that his works should not all men amaze?
Mumtáz [3] and Fu'ád [4] applaud and extol his every phrase,
Gazette [5] and Journal [6] both proclaim his doings aye.

Sharpen he but his wits anything whate'er to do,
In one or another way he is certain to pull it through,
E'en matters held by all for impossible hitherto.
Such is his might and power that if he but choose pursue,
Impossible things by scores to possibles changed will be. [7]

[1] That is this qasída called Zafer-Náme or Victory-Book, which Fázil Pasha is feigned to have written, and on which Khayrí Efendi is here supposed to be making a takhmís.

[2] زلف یاره طوقنمق 'To touch (caress) the locks of the beloved,' is a proverbial phrase meaning either to wound the susceptibilities of some one by touching his sore point, or, as here, to attack indirectly the policy of the government or of some great man. The phrase is quoted in the following couplet of Muníf:

زلف یاره طوقندی گیبی صبا   یینه بر پیچ وتاب وار دلده

"'Tis as though played the breeze with the loved one's locks,
'Once again is there qualm and throe in my heart.'

Ebu-z-Ziyá Tevfíq Bey, who cites this couplet in his book of proverbs, has followed a manuscript in which the last line of this distich has been transposed with the last line of the preceding one, the result being that the quotation, as he prints it, is meaningless. The preceding couplet, which is mystic, is:

ذرّة بیوجود عشقم لیك   صد هزار آفتاب وار دلده

'A mote inexistent of Love am I;
'Yet suns by the myriad glow in my heart.'

[3] Mumtáz Efendi, a government official of those days.

[4] Fu'ád Pasha, ᶜAlí's famous colleague.

[5] Taqwím-i Vaqáyiᶜ, the Ottoman official Gazette.

[6] Jeríde-i Hawádis, 'the Journal of Events', the well-known Constantinople paper with which so many of Ziyá's early associates were connected.

[7] Husní Pasha is made to say that this is of course a poetical exaggeration

'Tween him and the King of the Age [1] no sundering veil is spread; [2]
There is but this, that his name is not in the Khutbé read. [3]
But such is the power of his word in every spot and stead,
The Sultan is but a name on the tongue of the people said;
  The one who truly rules from the throne of the State is he.

The chief in Damascus town was by his orders slain; [4]

on the part of the author of the Zafer-Náme who by 'impossible things' means
things which none would have conceived possible of accomplishment, such
for instance, as this suppresion of a Cretan insurrection at the cost of only
some eighty thousand lives and a million or two of purses in so short a
time as two and a half years, or as the imprisonment and banishment of
many Musulmans without even the pretence of a trial, after the numerous
Imperial proclamations guaranteeing the liberty and the protection of the
lives, property and honour of all Ottoman subjects. Husní adds that Fázil
and Khayrí proceed in the following stanzas to give further examples of ⁽Alí
Pasha's successful accomplishment of other similar 'impossible things.'

[1] Sultan ⁽Abd-ul-⁽Azíz.

[2] I. e. ⁽Alí Pasha is on the most intimate terms with the Sultan whom he
has replaced, as the following lines declare, in the virtual sovereignty of the
Empire. 'It is among those impossible things which, through the power possessed by our lord ⁽Alí Pasha, have become possible, that he should subject
to himself a monarch so zealous of defending the rights of sovereignty as
Sultan ⁽Abd-ul-⁽Azíz.' (Commentary.)

[3] The Khutbé is the prayer recited in the mosques every Friday, in which
the name of the reigning sovereign is mentioned. Khayrí Efendi is here made
to say that the only distinction between the sovereignty of ⁽Abd-ul-⁽Azíz and
that of ⁽Alí Pasha is that the latter's name is not mentioned in this prayer.

[4] In the summer of ·1277 (1860) there was a serious riot in Damascus, in
the course of which many of the Christian inhabitants lost their lives. Pressure was brought to bear upon the Porte by certain of the European powers,
in consequence of which ⁽Alí's colleague, Fu'ád Pasha, was despatched to the
Syrian capital with instructions to put to death a number of the Muhammedan
inhabitants, including the governor Ahmed Pasha. This Ahmed Pasha was a
military officer who had served with distinction in the Crimea, and the shame-
ful treatment which, if Ziyá's account be correct, he received at the hands of
the Porte, culminating in his sacrifice to the bloodthirstiness of Europe, was
most likely the work of some high-placed rivals at head-quarters. This is
what Ziyá says through the mouth of Husní: 'This Wálí (Governor-General)
of Syria and Marshal of the ⁽Arabistán army-corps was the innocent and
martyred Ahmed Pasha. As is known to everyone, some three or four months
before the outbreak of the Damascus riot there were in that city four battalions of troops. At that time Ahmed Pasha was ordered by Rizá Pasha, the

then commander-in-chief, to despatch two of these with all speed to Rumelia Ahmed Pasha replied that owing to the intrigues of some foreign priests, and especially of the French consul in Damascus, signs of ill-feeling between the Muhammedan and Christian citizens had for some time been apparent, that it was difficult to maintain order even with the four battalions that he had, and that if the half of these were withdrawn, a tumult among the people was almost certain to occur. He added that should the despatch of these battalions be insisted on, he would pray that he might be allowed to resign his post and that another might be appointed thereto, as he would not be responsible for any evil results that might ensue. To these words Their Excellencies the Ministers paid not the slightest attention; they withdrew the battalions from Damascus and they did not replace Ahmed Pasha. Not long after this they demanded further one of the two battalions which still remained. Ahmed Pasha, who then foresaw what would happen, wrote an answer — a copy whereof was sent to the Imperial Palace and so must be lying pigeon-holed there — in which, after describing in an almost prophetic manner the disastrous events which would occur in Damascus, he categorically announced his resignation, as should this other battalion be withdrawn, he declared himself unable to preserve order in the city; while should his resignation be declined, he would none the less look upon himself as having resigned, as he would in no wise accept responsibility for the future. This reply was discussed in the cabinet, yet the battalion was withdrawn. Three or four days later the tumult broke out. The cry 'the Muhammedans are murdering the Christians!' made Europe jump up, and there was a tremendous uproar. Fu'ád Pasha was despatched, investigations were made, the upshot being that one hundred and sixty-eight innocent Muhammedans were executed, while they shot Ahmed Pasha, whom they reproached, saying, 'why did you not go out of the palace during the riot and let them tear you in pieces?' Requisitions were made on behalf of the Christian families who had suffered, and the Treasury indemnified them to the extent of 800,000 purses; and in such fashion was the matter closed. Many different reports were current concerning the execution of Ahmed Pasha; some people declared that on the occasion of a drunken quarrel between him and Fu'ád Pasha, when they were on service at Bucharest, Fu'ád said to Ahmed, 'Thy death shall be at my hands!' and in order to make good his words sacrificed him at Damascus. Others maintain that ʿAlí Pasha had for long borne ill-will to Ahmed Pasha, and, using this question as a pretext, brought about his death; and indeed when, during the course of the investigations, Ahmed Pasha was brought to Constantinople, ʿAlí Pasha urged his being sent back to Damascus, ostensibly for the completion of the investigation, but really, it is said, that he might complete the term of his life. Others again are of opinion that ʿAlí Pasha sacrificed Ahmed Pasha as a sop to Europe, and especially to the Emperor of the French; while, according to some, there was in addition to these reasons a rivalry for office between Rizá and Ahmed Pashas. But, be all this as it may, although the unfortunate Ahmed Pasha had fully and carefully instructed the

And thus did he heal the hates that clave the folk in twain. [1]

He granted the Nazarenes in the Lebanon to reign. [2]

government as to the state of affairs in his province, the authorities paid no attention to him, and the arms that he had and the troops that were with him were taken away, and he himself was afterwards shot. As our lord ʿAlí Pasha was then reigning supreme as Grand Vezir and Foreign Minister, the orders in these matters were executed at his instructions. Now before the occurrence of these events none would have believed it possible had it been said that such a state of affairs should arise, that a Marshal of the Ottoman Empire should be shot like a brigand, a sacrifice to the rancour of ʿAlí Pasha, that one hundred and sixty-eight Muhammedans should be butchered, and that several hundreds of households should be driven into exile, and their women and children left to perish. Yet the might of our lord ʿAlí Pasha has brought these seemingly impossible occurrences into the field of possibility!'

[1] This line is of course ironical, racial and religious enmity not being extinguishable by the blood of any number of Wális.

[2] In consequence of continued fighting between the Druses and Maronites, a body of French troops under General Hautpoul and of Turkish troops under Fu'ád Pasha marched upon Mount Lebanon in the autumn of 1860. Later on the district was, through French influence, formed into a separate province, the governor of which must be a Roman Catholic, that is, a co-religionist of the Maronites. Here is Ziyá's account of the business as given through the Commentary: 'Another instance of the power of our lord ʿAlí Pasha to make possible the impossible is the placing of the government of the Lebanon in the hands of a member of the Catholic sect. As is generally known, until the question of the Lebanon arose, those parts were under the administration of the governors of Sidon and Beyrút. The inhabitants of the Mountain are of two peoples of different religions who are called Druses and Maronites. The Maronites are Catholics, and so they have always had the moral support of France; but as the Druses, who have a special creed of their own, are the more numerous, they are unable to put up with the privileges of the Maronites. Consequently there is never any cessation of strife and quarreling between them; the more especially as the Catholic priests, seeking to drive the Druses into the Catholic sect, and the French consuls, hoping some day to annex those districts to France like Algiers, never leave off exciting hostility between the two peoples. At length, after the trouble in the Lebanon, it was decided to give over the government of those parts entirely over to the Catholics by placing the administration in the hands of a mushír who must belong to that sect. A number of privileges were also granted which do not prevail in other provinces. The governorship, along with the rank of mushír, was conferred first on Dáwud Efendi, who had been chargé d'affaires at Berlin and had written a book in the German language, and who was moreover one of the most steadfast in obedience and humility among

In Egypt-land a change in the heirs did he ordain. [1]
He made a captain Prince of Roumania to be. [2]

Ten thousand Muslim households, obeying his command,
Abandoned hearth and homestead and fled their native land.
That there should float our banner — with this condition grand —
To Servia the fortress of Belgrade did he hand: [3]
Thus perfectly he preserved the Empire's integrity! [4]

Alí Pasha's servants. But after some years certain indications of thoughts of independence were perceived in him, so he was brought under a clever pretext to Constantinople, and the notorious Franco Efendi, one of Fu'ád Pasha's sycophants, was made mushír and appointed governor of the Mountain in his stead. As Maronites and Druses alike are savage mountaineers, honest and trustworthy men are exceedingly rare among them; while very plentiful are the likes of Rizq-ulláh Hasún, who, while chief secretary of the tobacco customs, was for well-known reasons put in prison, whence he escaped and took up his abode with his compatriot Ghadbán, the Ottoman consul in London. Now before these events would it have been thought possible that the Mountain should have been thus placed under a practically independent government which is virtually under the control of France? But lo, the might of our lord ªAlí Pasha has achieved this !'

[1] Direct succession to the Khedivial throne was granted in 1866 to the Viceregal family of Egypt, in place of the Ottoman system which had prevailed since the time of Mehemmed ªAlí Pasha. By the change thus effected, Mustafá Fázil Pasha, Ziyá's former patron, lost his chance of succession; and it is in the commentary on this line of the Zafer-Náme that the poet takes his revenge on his faithless friend, by making Husní bring forward many charges against him ostensibly to justify ªAlí Pasha in sanctioning this change in the succession on the ground of Mustafá Fázil's being an imbecile and consequently unfit to reign.

[2] Prince Charles of Hohenzollern-Sigmaringen, elected in 1866.

[3] The Imperial government maintained a garrison in the citadel of Belgrade till 1867, when the troops were withdrawn, and the fortress handed over to the Servians. It was stipulated that the Ottoman flag should continue to fly over the citadel, — a barren recognition of the Sultan's suzerainty which the Servians did not very long respect. The first two lines of the stanza refer to the Muhammedan inhabitants of Belgrade, who, unable to trust the native government, had to leave their homes when the troops that had hitherto protected them were withdrawn.

[4] Referring to the oft quoted phrase 'the integrity and independence of the Ottoman Empire.'

The Kenez, [1] too, hath been brought by his words to the rightful way,
No more will he pounce as of old to left and right on his prey;
In a realm so safe as that what need for a guard to stay?
What though in Montenegro he did the forts away!
A gnat can a mount o'erthrow, if the will of God it be! [2]

If but the help of God assist in his purpose dear,
Full soon will these gypsies sit on the couch of the Grand Vezír;
It is but the Jews alone that form the exception here, [3]

[1] The Kenez (sometimes pronounced Kinz) is the title given by the Turks to the Prince of Montenegro. Formerly, when that savage chieftain exercised the functions of an ecclesiastical as well as of a temporal ruler, he was called the Ladiqa. Both Kenez (Knyaz) and Ladiqa are originally Slavonic words.

[2] In the commentary on this stanza we read: 'As is well known, this Montenegrin business, during the four years that it lasted, swallowed up the pick of the Ottoman officers and soldiers and the bravest youths of Bosnia and Herzegovina, was the cause of the present desolation of these two provinces, and inflicted on the Treasury a loss of many thousand purses. At the same time it was the making of certain men who, though previously unknown, have now come to the front; Kání Pasha, Dervísh Pasha and their likes have fattened on the soup of that free-kitchen, but it is in the blood of many thousands of the Muslims that they have broken their bread. At length the mountainers were overcome, and the Muslim troops entered Cettigne. On this the Sublime Porte conferred with the Five Powers, and it was unanimously agreed that block-houses built of stone should be erected in such places as were necessary in Montenegro and garrisoned with a sufficient number of troops, in order to protect the adjacent Ottoman territories from further depredations by the inhabitants of that country, as these know not of such matters as trade and agriculture, and have no other occupation than brigandage and highway robbery. Now although the mountaineers, through their native savagery, used during the war to cut off the ears and noses of our soldiers, and to rip up the slain and tear out their entrails, and had indeed formed at Cettigne a regular museum of the heads of our soldiers, yet as they represented to our lord His Highness ᶜAlí Pasha, through the medium of the Russian embassy, that the decision to build such block-houses was very distressful to them, and that so long as they saw these before their eyes a certain coolness might overtake the loyalty they were all eager to bestow upon their Suzerain, and as the French embassy supported the Russian by friendly advice, the pity and compassion of our lord the Pasha were excited, and all those block-houses, bought with the blood of so many thousand Muslim soldiers and at the cost of so many thousand purses, were levelled with the ground.'

[3] When Ziyá wrote, no Jew had ever been promoted to the grade of Bálá or Mushír.

For of Greeks and Armenians both doth he make Bey and Mushír;
   The equality of rights [1] to perfection brought hath he. [2]

*   *   *

Though the purpose of Fu'ád was to win at Damascus fame,
What need a wholesale slaughter of the Muslims to proclaim? [3]
Were 't not enow had he acted like him of noble name? [4]
Such are the deeds they do who at lasting glory aim;
   Is 't meet to defile Zemzem though one would remembered be? [5]

Were it strange at all that he [6] who doth Fortune's charger ride,
When armed with the whip of zeal, should the wall like a donkey guide, [7]
What else could have brought such weal within so brief a tide?
Had ever the steed of Empire so swift unto progress hied,
   Had he not urged it on with the spur of his energy?

[1] The equality of rights between the different races subject to the Sultan.

[2] This stanza is followed by three in which ʿAlí Pasha's financial arrangements are criticised.

[3] A return to Fu'ád Pasha and the Damascus executions.

[4] That is, Fu'ád should have acted at Damascus as ʿAlí did in Crete.

[5] Referring to a legend of a certain filthy and foolish fellow who defiled the Zemzem, the sacred well at Mekka, in the hope that by thus doing what none had ever done before, he might immortalize his name. 'And in truth, because of that villainy of his, will the name of that accursed one be mentioned with execration while the world lasts. * * * * The writer of the poem, attributing Fu'ád Pasha's proceedings in Ḍamascus to a desire to perpetuate his name, compares him to the fellow who defiled the Zemzem; the humble commentator would say that as Yezíd is also, like the defiler of the Zemzem, amongst those who have made a name at Damascus, it would have been most appropriate to have compared the Pasha to him. Alas, that the metre would not admit of it!' The Yezíd here mentioned was the son and successor of the usurping Caliph Muʿáwiya, and is loathed and execrated above all others by the Muslims; indeed he holds in the Muhammedan world much the place occupied by Judas Iscariot in the Christian. It was by his orders that the martyrs of Kerbelá were slain, and it was he who most cruelly insulted the hapless survivors of that fatal day when brought into his presence at Damascus. One Muslim can cast no more bitter reproach at another than to compare him to Yezíd.

[6] I. e. ʿAlí Pasha.

[7] A reference to a legend concerning the saint Hajji Bektásh, which says that when that holy man desired to go from one place to another he used to mount a wall which carried him whither he would be.

To his private audience none may win who is base or low
He doth on the ‘ulemá whate’er they desire bestow.
No scorn of the Prophet's race would he in public show;
So great a lord is he, did the Dean of the Sherífs [1] go
    Up to his audience-hall, his place would the shoe-rank be. [2]

The Arab and Persian Kings are eclipsed by his high renown;
The titles of royalty he appropriates as his own,
By the style of Son Altesse in the Moniteurs he is known. [3]
Is it much though to Europe's lands his eagle-fame is flown?
    Were it strange should a vulture fly to Beyqoz from Geybize? [4]

Should he but his holy ire to the raging lion show,
Its body would fall in bits for the dread it were sure to know,
So let not the evil beasts in heedless surety go;
As yet they have felt not his wrath, but should they once do so,
    Not a wolf would the mountain roam, not a mouse o'er the ceiling flee!

Although he may harshly deal with the righteous men and wise,
'Tis but as a father acts when he doth his son chastise.
For alum from sugar well enough can he recognize. [5]

---

[1] The Naqíb-ul-Eshráf or Dean of the Sherífs, the registrar of the descendants of the Prophet in a province or city. The Dean of the Sherífs for
Constantinople is a much venerated official.

[2] The shoe-rank (saff-i ni‘ál) is the place by the door of an Oriental room
where shoes are left on entering and where servants wait. See Browne's remarks
on this subject in the *J. R. A. S.* for 1895, pp. 805—808.

[3] By the 'Moniteurs' the European press is meant.

[4] Beyqoz is a village on the Bosphorus, Geybize is a small town between
Scutari and Izmid. 'The humble commentator would say that if the comparison
of the passage of our benefactor's fame into Europe to the flight of a vulture
from Geybize to Beyqoz appear somewhat vulgar, this results from the fact
that the author of the poem is a provincial. As is well known:
    "Never is the country beauty dainty, e'en though fair she be." '
It will be borne in mind that the pseudo-author of the Zafer-Náme qasída
is Fázil Pasha the Bosnian. The line Husní is made to quote is from a ghazel
of Nábí : —

كنارك دلبرى نازكده اولسه نازنين اولماز

شاب ايله شكرى فرق ايدر [5] 'He can tell between alum and sugar,'
is a proverb.

Full many a fair and cultured home would he pulverize,
  Did not his noble heart incline towards clemency.

The Turkish virtues old are all, alack, undone;
The ancient Turkish zeal abideth in ne'er an one;
The Turkish glory of yore is past away and gone;
The Turkish State is come into such a plight that none
  The signs and portents sad of approaching doom can see.

Though to show what is naught as aught doth no little talent need,
Harder yet than the juggle is to get it believed indeed. [1]
For all that many a hap hath occurred the work to speed,
What skill is thine that it doth these twenty years succeed
  In cheating Europe still and deceiving the world alway! [2]

The King of earth unto thee subjected boweth low;
Supreme in his name thou'st ruled since many a year ago.
All manner of wonderment and amaze were it meet to show.
How happy-starred, for so long, with all the world thy foe,
  To sit all uncontrolled on the throne of mastery!

No longer confiding now in thy promises full fair,
Regarding thy notions wise as though they but follies were,
And seeking each evil plight to thee alone to refer,
At thee swear the Muslims all, and at thee non-Muslims swear;
  Alack, there is never an one who knoweth the worth of thee!

Relying on thine indulgence, extended to those who claim,
Fázil [3] hath sung thy lauds, while Khayrí [4] details the same:
(Never did he when young vituperate thee or blame.) [5]
Although in his dotage, still will Fázil they praise proclaim;
  Though his teeth be gone, will the dog of race still of service be. [6]

---

[1] Difficult as the actual juggle is, it is yet more difficult so to execute it that people may never guess there has been any juggle at all.

[2] From this stanza the poem is addressed directly to 'Alí Pasha.

[3] Old Fázil Pasha the Bosnian, the pretended author of the Zafer-Náme qasída.

[4] Khayrí Efendi, the pretended author of the Takhmís on the Zafer-Náme.

[5] From this it seem that Fázil at one time opposed 'Alí, which Khayrí here takes credit to himself for never having done.

[6] صوى كوپك ديشلرى دوكولسهده صالـديـرر 'The dog of race will attack even when his teeth are gone,' is a proverb. 'The humble commentator

Wan was my [1] face and pale for dejeation and despair,[2]
And ever the tribe of duns would pluck at my beard and hair;[3]
Belike with this torment dure the reels full wounden were;[4]
A mutesarrifship through a qit‘a became my share;[5]
So this qasída[6] should win a wáliship[7] for me.[8]

would say: When Fázil Pasha, curbing his pride, compares himself for fidelity
o a dog, he must mean either a sporting dog or one of those that guard
the flocks and vineyards. For such dogs, even when they have lost their
teeth, and can no longer chase away wolves and thieves, do not sit idle,
they at least howl. Similarly, Fázil Pasha, being a man of good family, though
no longer in full possession of his senses, does not cease from making verses,
good or bad, in praise and honour of our benefactor.'

[1] Although Khayrí is still the pretended author of the takhmís, Fázil is
the supposed speaker throughout the whole of this and the following stanzas.

[2] A reference to the proverb, بورجلو اولنز بگزی صارارر 'the debtor dies
not, but his face grows pale.'

[3] Referring to a time when Fázil Pasha was out of office and hard pressed
by his creditors, Husní proceeds: 'The (once) debt-laden commentator would
say that the importunity of duns is indeed intolerable. When I was out of
office I learned the taste of it. But now, since, thank God, I have become a
Marshal, I have been delivered from that torment, not indeed through saving
from my salary and paying my debts, but by appointing some of my creditors
keepers or wardens at the prisons, and by employing others as spies or
members of the secret police.'

[4] چلهسی طولدی 'The reel thereof is filled' is a proverb which we might
paraphrase by 'the cup of misery has run over.'

[5] Referring to the mutesarrifship of Izmid which Fázil held, and which
Ziyá would have us believe was conferred on him by ‘Alí Pasha on his
composing a qit‘a (here referred to) on Ziyá's flight to Europe.

[6] This qasída, i. e. the Zafer-Náme.

[7] A wáliship, i. e. the governor-generalship of a vilájet or province, which
comprises several mutesarrifships.

[8] Not desiring to be overlooked when there is a question of favours being
conferred, the 'humble commentator' thus delivers himself here: 'The humble
commentator would say: It is not too much to hope for a wáliship in
recompense of a brilliant qasída like the Zafer-Náme from that source of
bounty which rewarded a qit‘a of four lines with the mutesarrifship of Izmid.
Since it is the usage of poets, at the end of a qasída just before the prayer,
to crave some boon from him whom they praise, the author of the poem here
requests that he may be provided for with a wáliship, while the portionless
commentator will confine himself to a little hint to that benign physician,
namely to the gracious, belauded Sublime one (a play on the name ‘Alí or
Sublime), that the attack of the itch wherefrom he is suffering might be

As the month of May is the tide of health (so physicians say),
For them who would blessings crave the time is the dawn of day; [1]
So now let us to the Lord with loyal devotion pray.
Desist from thy toil and moil, and cast thy reed away,
  And Mekka-ward bow thy head with all sincerity. [2]

So long as the Salamander in his fiery dwelling lies,
So long as the Phœnix doth from his ashes heavenward rise,
So long as the Stellar Eagle [3] circling and soaring flies,
So long as Humá and Símurgh do wing them through the skies.
  May the partridge of his pomp 'scape the hawk of adversity!

May nothing that is or is not e'er his noble heart offend, [4]

cured by a decoration set with jewels. That Khayrí Efendi is entitled to ask for some favour on account of his takhmís is self-evident, but the exigencies of metre have prevented him from making any request; there is, however, no doubt that he too will get his desire through the channel of His Highness's sons.' Husní Pasha is elsewhere made to hint at his eagerness for a decoration (presumably the Mejídiyye, since the 'Osmániyye order was not instituted until 1288 = A. D. 1871—2). Thus when speaking, in the commentary on a preceding untranslated stanza, on the usual penuriousness and jealousy of poets, he says: 'As the present writer likewise (though he has no claim thereto) is reckoned among the poets, for all that he is Marshal of Police, he has been unable to escape from penuriousness, and although there is no jealousy in his soul, yet were he to say that he feels no pangs when he sees ministers on whose breasts is the decoration in question, he would tell a lie.'

[1] The old poets used to say that the prayers uttered at dawn were the most effectual.

[2] In these two lines the poet addresses himself. The two stanzas which follow, which are the last of the poem, contain the prayer for ʿAlí Pasha's prosperity.

[3] That is the constellation Aquila; it will noticed that they are all fabulous animals the continuance of whose existence is to be the measure of ʿAlí Pasha's spell of prosperity.

[4] 'The humble commentator would say that seeing how as it is impossible that the heart of any man, so long as he is in this world, should always be free from every actual or possible trouble, to express such a wish concerning one is a polite way of expressing a desire that he may depart to the Hereafter; but that the intention of the author of the poem must be to declare his hope that the ears of our lord ʿAlí Pasha may be strong.' 'May the ears of So-and-so be strong' is a whimsical way of praying that he may continue to enjoy good health.

And him may God exempt from the spite of the envious band! [1]
While e'en as his stature, far may ever his shade extend! [2]
And like to his boundless grace, may his lifetime know no end!
And great as his pity is, may his fortune and favour be!

[1] 'Seeing that so long as man lives he is an object of envy, and that so long as he is an object of envy he is exposed to spite, exemption from the envier's spite is only possible with death. But the author of the poem means that His Highness ʿAlí Pasha ought not to be worried.' (Commentary.)

[2] ʿAlí Pasha was short of stature.

(Here ends the Author's manuscript. The continuation and completion of the book, undertaken by a Turkish man of letters, will form the seventh and concluding volume of the work.)

E. G. B.

INDEX I.

NAMES OF PERSONS AND PLACES, ETC.

Ahmed, personal name of Nedím, IV 30.

Ahmed, hero of Yahyá Bey's *Sháh u Gedá*, III 123.

Ahmed (old Turkish poet), I 225, 226, 260, 427.

Ahmed, Prince, son of Báyezíd II, II 125, 129, 135, 228, 257, 259, 266, 367.

Ahmed I, Sultan, I 417 n. 1; III 2, 165, 201, 205 sqq., 209, 252, 263.

Ahmed II, Sultan, III 233 n. 1, 302.

Ahmed III, Sultan, I 417 n. 1; II 142 n. 1; III 2, 155 n. 3, 202, 205, 233 n. 1, 245; IV 3, 4, 8, 11 sqq., 24, 29-31, 37, 53, 61, 67, 75, 77 n. 5, 81, 88, 107, 108, 110 sqq., 243, 279.

Ahmed, Sultan, Mosque of, I 237 n. 2.

Ahmed Bey, V 43 seq.

Ahmed-i Bíján, I 396 sqq., 406.

Ahmed Burhán-ud-Din. See Burhán-ud-Dín, Cadi.

Ahmed-i Dácí, I 211, 249, 253, 256 seq.

Ahmed Dede, IV 37 n. 1.

Ahmed Jeláyirí, Sultan, I 207 n. 2.

Ahmed Midhat Efendi, V 13.

Ahmed-i Misrí, I 430 n. 1; V 13 n. 1.

Ahmed Mukhtár Efendi, III 171; IV 151, 349.

Ahmed Neylí Efendi. See Neylí.

Ahmed Pasha, the poet, I 128, 228—230, 231 n. 1, 416; II 10, 16, 18, 25, 31, 32, 40 sqq., 85, 88 n. 2, 93, 94, 95, 104, 106, 109, 123, 229, 230 n. 1, 277, 284, 288, 365, 368, 371, 388; III 53, 85, 179 n. 2, 325; IV 99; V 32, 80, 82.

Ahmed Pasha, ex-governor of Baghdád, IV 93.

Ahmed Pasha, governor of Damascus, V 101 n. 4.

Ahmed Pasha, governor of Salonica, III 294.

Ahmed el-Qudúrí, IV 342.

Ahmed Rátib Pasha, IV 125 n. 3.

Ahmed Reficá Efendi, IV 211.

Ahmed bin Shemsí, personal name of cAhdí, III 8.

Ahmed, Sheykh, I 304 n. 1.

Ahmed Vefíq Pasha, V 14, 15, Ahmed Wásif Efendi IV 279 n. 1.

Ahmed-i Yeseví, I 71, 76, 92, 95, 104, 169.

Ahmedí, I 108, 211, 228, 253, 255, **260** sqq., 299, 308, 311, 336, 414, 427, 429, 436, 443, 444; II 19, 51, 52, 200, 377; III 86, 171 n. 1.

Al-Ahqáf, I 326 n. 5.

Ahriman, V 89 n. 2.

Akbar, Sultan, III 190 n. 4.

10

Selím Giráy, Khán of the Crimea, IV 21.

Selím the Martyr. See Selím III, Sultan.

Selím, Prince, afterwards Selím I, II 257 seq., 318, 367.

Selím, Prince, afterwards Selím II, III 8.

Selím I, Sultan, I 204 n. 2, 257 n. 1, 262 n. 2, 417 n. 1; II 29, 30, 86, 172 n. 3, 228, 238, 257 sqq., 266 sqq., 276, 277, 288, 290, 319, 320 n. 8, 325, 329, 347, 352, 356, 358, 364, 369, 370, 374 n. 2, 384, 391, 395; III 12, 17, 25, 42—44, 48, 49, 62 n. 1, 86, 88, 160, 162 n. 4, 167, 262; V 80.

Selím II, Sultan, I 257 n. 1, 417 n. 1; III 5, 8, 10, 11, 108, 109, 134, 151, 165, 167, 171, 206, 233.

Selím III, Sultan, I 417 n. 1; IV 151, 161 n. 2, 178 seq., 221 sqq., 226, 245, 350; V 4, 20.

Selímí, pen-name of Sultan Selím II, I 417 n. 1.

Seljúqs, the, I 10 seq., 141; IV 311.

Selmán, Khʾája. See Selmán-i Sávejí.

Selmán, Mír. See Mír Selmán.

Selmán-i Sávejí, Persian poet, I 285, 286; II 72, 291; III 79, 139, 179 n. 5.

Selsebíl, a river of Paradise,

I 36; III 76 n. 2, 317 n. 1; IV 52 n. 1, 112 n. 6.

Semáʿí, pen-name of Sultan Díwání, I 424 n. 1.

Senáʾí, Hakím, I 428.

Senáʾí of Qastamuni, II 368.

Seraglio, the, name of a palace, II 58.

Seraglio Point, II 26, 45 n. 1.

Serendíb, I 275.

Seres, I 228; II 72 n. 7, 73 n. 2.

Serkis, IV 94 n. 1.

Serpents, King of the, I 433.

Serpents, Queen of the, I 433 n. 2.

Servia, IV 259; V 97 n. 2.

Servili (Cypress-Inn), name of a tavern, V 56.

Sevdáʾí, II 172 n. 3, 377.

Seven Sleepers, the, of Ephesus, V 79.

Seven Towers, Castle of the, II 43 n. 1.

Seven Towers, Gate of the, III 180.

Seyf-ul-Mulk, I 439.

Seyf-ul-Mulúk, I 439 n. 1.

Seyyid ʿImád, a name given to Nesímí, I 351.

Seyyid-i Sheríf, title of ʿAlí-i Jurjání, II 349 n. 3.

Seyyid Vehbí. See Vehbí, Seyyid.

Sganarelle, V 14.

Shaʿbán, the dynasty of, IV 226 seq.

of Nesh'et, IV 211, 276 n. 3.

Suleymán-i Burseví, I 232. See Suleymán Chelebi.

Suleymán Chelebi, I 108, 225, 228, **232** sqq., 268, 307, 308, 392, 399, 415; II 51, 190, 191; III 54; V 77.

Suleymán Dede, I 232 n. 1. See Suleymán Chelebi.

Suleymán Fá'iq Efendi, IV 245.

Suleymán, Mír. See Mír Suleymán.

Suleymán Nahífí. See Nahífí.

Suleymán Pasha, I 411.

Suleymán, Prince, son of Báyezíd I, I 249, 250, 252, 255—257, 259 n. 1, 260, 263, 265, 267, 269, 285, 287, 297, 417, 427, 428; III 334 n. 1.

Suleymán Sháh, (father of Ertoghrul, the first Sultan of the Ottomans), I 10, 141.

Suleymán Sháh, a member of the royal house of Germiyan, I 423 seq.

Suleymán I, Sultan, I 140 n. 1, 204 n. 2, 358; II 21, 25 n. 2, 239 n. 4, 257, 347, 352, 358, 376, 395, 399 seq.; III 1 sqq., 25, 27, 36, 49, 59, 63, 71 n. 2, 72, 75, 83, 86, 106, 108, 118, 119, 123, 123, 126, 133, 134, 136, 146, 147, 151 sqq., 161, 163, 166, 169, 186, 204—206, 233; V 80.

Suleymán II, Sultan, III 302; IV 15, 21.

Suleymáníye Mosque, the, II 399; V 45.

Sulmán, Mír. See Mír Selmán.

Sultan Ahmed, the Mosque of, I 237 n. 2.

Sultan Ahmed el-Jeláyirí, I 207 n. 2.

Sultan Díwání, mystic, I 424 n. 1.

Sultan Mehemmed the Conqueror. See Mehemmed II, Sultan.

Sultan Murád, the Mosque of, II 82.

Sultan Orkhan, College of, at Izniq, III 41.

Sultan Shujá', mystic, I 413.

Sultán Veled, I 108, 141, **151** sqq., 168, 185, 210, 213, 235, 268, 308, 421, 423; II 7, 14.

Sultan Yildirim Khan, I 256 n. 1.

Sultána Mihr-u-Máh, College of III 172.

Sultan-öni, II 47.

Sunbul-záde, patronymic, IV 242.

Sunbul-záde Vehbí, I 86; III 272 n. 2, 334; IV 108, 110, 119, 124 **242** sqq., 267, 268, 271, 272, 289 n. 3, 302 n. 1, 336; V 47 n. 1, 52, 65.

Sun'í, II 97, 99 n. 1, 101, 366 n. 1.

Yezdejird, Yezdigird, I 269; III 365 seq.

Yezíd ibn Mu'áwiya, the Caliph, III 91; IV 246 n. 2; V 93 n. 4, 94 n. 4, 106 n. 5.

Yildirim Báyezíd (Báyezíd the Thunderbolt), I 231 n. 1, 249. See Báyezíd I, Sultan.

Yildirím Khan, Sultan, I 256 n. 1.

Yoraki (George), name of a dancing-boy, IV 236.

Yorgi Dandini, V 14.

Yúnán (Ionia), I 149 n. 1, 177 n. 5, 178 n. 1, 270.

Yúnus Imre, I 141, 164 sqq., 185, 204 n. 3, 226 n. 1.

Yúnus Pasha, II 228.

Yúsuf, author of the *Qudatqu Bilik*, I 71.

Yúsuf (Joseph), name of a boy, II 254 n. 1.

Yúsuf, name of Nábí, III 325.

Yúsuf, the Prophet. See Joseph.

Yúsuf, surnamed Sína-chák, III 61 n. 3.

Yúsuf Kámil Pasha, V 13, 25, 27.

Yuzghad, IV 324.

Zábulistán, I 272 n. 1.

Zacharias, V 92 n. 1.

Za'fí, II 375.

Zahák, III 266 n. 6.

Záhid, son of Sultan Veled, I 422.

Zahír-ud-Dín Fáryábí, I 144, 285, 286; III 139, 179 n. 5.

Zál, father of Rustem, II 300 n. 2; IV 48 n. 2; V 96 n. 1.

Zamírí, II 369.

Zanzibar, III 266 n. 3.

Zarífí Efendi, III 108.

Zátí, I 107; II 52, 106, 128 n. 2, 149, 229, 244 n. 7, 321; III 47 sqq., 108, 109, 135 seq., 138 n. 1, 181, 182, 206, 237 n. 2, 354; V 80, 82.

Zehir-Már-záde, sobriquet of Rizá, III 202.

Zekeriyyá, the Muslim form of Zacharias, III 273 n. 2.

Zekeriyyá Efendi, III 273, 276.

Zelíkhá, Potiphar's wife, I 168 n. 1; II 12, 64 n. 1, 142 sqq., 157 sqq.; III 31 n. 1, 55 n. 1, 236.

Zemzem, IV 111 n. 10; V 106 n. 5.

Zengís (Abyssinians), the, III 359.

Zeresb, I 272 n. 1.

Zeyd, an unfortunate lover, II 188 sqq.

Zeyn-ul-'Abidín, son of Burhán-ud-Dín, I 206.

Zeyn-ul-'Areb, Sheykh, I 392, 403.

Zeyn-ud-Dín, son of the poet Hamdí, II 141.

Zeyn-ud-Dín-i Háfí, Sheykh, I 139.

Zeyneb, cousin of Zeyd, II 188.

12

INDEX II.

BOOKS, JOURNALS, POEMS, ETC.

A.

Academy, the, III 326 n. 1.
ᶜAdam Qasídasi (the Qasída of Nothingness), IV 329 sqq.
Advice, a Mother's — to her Daughter, IV 285 n. 1.
Ahádís (Traditional Sayings of the Prophet), collected and translated by Báqí, III 146.
Ahmediyye of Hamdí, II 199.
Ahmed u Mahmúd of Zátí, III 50, 53.
ᶜAjáᵓib-ul-Makhlúqát (Marvels of Creation) of Qazwíní, translated by Ahmed-i Bíján, I 392, 406.
Akhláq-i ᶜAláᵓí (the Exalted Ethics), I 41 n. 1; II 45.
Akhláq-i Jeláli, II 28 n. 1.
Akhter, Persian newspaper, I 359 n. 1.
ᵛAlem-numá (World-Displayer), title of ᶜAtáᵓí's *Sáqi-Náme,* III 235.
Alfiyya u Shalfiyya, III 37.
Ancient Arabian Poetry, III 174 n. 3.
Anemone, the Blood-red, III 41 n. 3. See *Peony, the Crim-* son and *Shaqáᵓiq-un-Nuᶜmániyya.*
Antimachus of Colophon and the Position of Women in Greek Poetry, I 64 n. 2.
Anvár-i Suheylí (Lights of Canopus), III 90 n. 1.
Arabian Nights, the, I 274 n. 1, 331 n. 7, 432 sqq.; II 113 n. 6, 331 n. 4; III 175 n. 1; IV 48 n. 3; V 13.
ᶜArsh-Náme (The Book of the Throne), I 337, 376, 385 n. 5.
Art of Poetry, the, by Puttenham, IV 273 n. 1.
ᵛAshiq Pasha Díwáni (Díwán of ᵛAshiq Pasha), I 183 n. 1,
ᵛAshiq u Maᶜshúq, mesneví wrongly attributed to Zátí, III 50 n. 1.
Ass and the Fox, Fable of the, V 33, 36 sqq.
ᵓAtesh-Kede (The Fire-Temple), IV 247 n. 1.
Athenaeum, the, I 152 n. 1.
ᶜAzliyya, name of a qasída by Nábí, III 332.

Ottoman Sultans, History of the, by Bihishtí, II 376 n. 1.
Ottomans, History of the, by Kemál-Pasha-záde, II 358.
Our Poetesses, by Ahmed Mukhtár Efendi, IV 151, 349. See *Shá'ir Khánimlarimiz*.

P.

Pend-Náme (Book of Counsels), by Guwáhí, II 124.
Penj Genj (Five Treasures), of Nizámí, III 365.
Pentateuch, the, I 375 n. 2, 376; II 105 n. 2.
Peony, the Crimson, I 262, 263, 264, 265, 299, 300, 380, 390, 406, 413 n. 1; II 44 n. 1, 139 n. 1, 140 n. 2, 141 n. 2, 148, 174, 190, 199, 273 n. 2, 276, 348, 354; III 140, 162 n. 4, 171, 233. See *Shaqá'iq-un-Nu'mániyya*.
Persians, a Year amongst the, I 15 n. 1, 62 n. 1; II 46 n. 2, 334 n. 7, 336 n. 1, 340 n. 1, 341 n. 8; IV 172 n. 3, 225 n. 1, 293 n. 1.
Poems, the Suspended, III 174 n. 3. See *Mu'allaqát*.
Poeseos Asiaticae commentariorum libri sex, II 232 n. 1.
Posy from the Garths of Culture, by Belígh of Brusa, IV 117. See *Guldeste-i Riyáz-i 'Irfán*.
Professor's Magazine, by

Nájí, III 50. See *Mejmú'a-i Mu'allim*.
Psalms, the, I 375 n. 2, 376; II 105 n. 2; III 18 n. 1, 191 n. 3, 215 n. 2.

Q.

Qábús-Náma, III 334.
Qahramán-Náma, III 149 n. 6.
Qánún-Náme (Book of Laws), II 21.
Qámús, the, I 121; IV 231, 248 n. 1; V 22, 65, 75.
Qasída-i 'Azliyya (The Deposal Qasída), III 342.
Qasída, the Hyacinth, III 133.
Qasída-i Tannána (The Resonant Qasída), IV 244, 249 sqq., 264.
Qasída-i Tayyára (The Volant Qasída), IV 245, 249 sqq.
Qasídet-ul-Burde (The Mantle-Poem), IV 82.
Qastamuni-Náme (Qastamuni-Book), II 108; III 161.
Qirq Vezír Ta'ríkhi (The History of the Forty Vezírs), V 13 n. 1. See *Forty Vezírs, History of the.*
Qudatqu Bilik (The Auspicious Knowledge), I 71, 78, 104 seq.

R.

Raqqás-Náme (Book of Dancers), IV 235 n. 2.

13

INDEX III.

Index of Technical Terms and Oriental Words.

'Abá-i Seb^ca (The Seven Sires), I 48.

^cAbír, unguent, I 334 n. 3.

^cAdam (not-being), IV 330. See Not-being.

^cAdan, Arabic name for Eden and Aden, III 300 n. 2.

'Aghá (sergeant), III 364.

'Ahenk (harmony), V 48 n. 2.

^cAjil, II 345 n. 5.

Akásira, plural of Kisrá, III 148 n. 6.

Akhlát-i erba^ca (the four humours), I 301 n. 1. See Humours, the four.

^cAks (Antistrophe), I 115.

'Al (red), II 239 n. 2.

'Al (family), II 239 n. 2.

^cAlem (The Universe), I 41.

^cAlem-i 'Ab (The World Aquose), IV 106 n. 1.

^cAlem-i A^cyán-i Sábita (The World of the Fixed Prototypes), I 55.

^cAlem-i Berzakh (The Intermediate World), I 55.

^cAlem-i Ghayb (The Invisible World), I 56.

^cAlem-i Hissí (The Sensible World), I 56 n. 1.

^cAlem-i Insán (The World of Man), I 56.

^cAlem-i Jeberút (The World of Might), I 55.

^cAlem-i Kevn u Fesád (The World of Generation and Corruption), I 56 n. 1.

^cAlem-i Kubrá (The Greater World or Macrocosm), I 62.

^cAlem-i Láhút (The World of Godhead), I 55.

^cAlem-i Ma^cání (The World of Meanings), I 55 n. 2.

^cAlem-i Melekút (The Angel World), I 55, 56.

^cAlem-i Misál (The World of Similitudes), I 55.

^cAlem-i Mulk (The World of the Kingdom), I 56, 188 n. 2.

^cAlem-i Shehádet (The Visible World), I 55, 56.

^cAlem-i Sughrá (The Lesser World or Microcosm), I 62.

^cAlem-i Súret (The World of Form), I 56 n. 1.

'Al-i ^cAbá (The Family of the Cloak), III 105 n. 2.

^cAlim (Knower), name of God, I 409 n. 1.

Alláhu Ekber, II 244 n. 2.

Altmishlu, class of *muderris*, II 398.

Altun, name of a coin, II 26 n. 2.

'Amedji, the office of, IV 324.

Anadoli Muhásibejisi (Auditor for Anatolia), III 326.

Anóshak-rúbán, title, II 63 n. 4. See Núshírewán.

Aq, used as a sobriquet, II 138 n. 1.

Aqcha, name of a coin, I 262 n. 2.

Aqcha-i ʿOsmání, I 262 n. 2.

ʿAql (Reason), I 197 n. 2; II 389 n. 1.

ʿAql-i Evvel (First Intelligence), I 42. See Intelligence, the Primal ; Logos.

ʿAql-i Faʿʿál (Active Intelligence), I 43; III 356.

ʿAql-i Kull (Universal Intelligence), I 42. See *ʿAql-i Evvel.*

ʿAql-i Mahjúb (Veiled Reason), II 199 n. 1.

ʿAql-i Nefsání (Carnal Reason), III 128 n. 5.

'Aqá-yi Seyyid, nickname of hashísh, II 340 n. 1.

ʿAraba (coach), IV 314.

ʿAraq (spirit), III 89 n. 2.

ʿAraz (Accident), I 41.

Arpa Emini (Intendant of the Barley), IV 58.

ʿArsh (Throne of God), I 35, 68, 172 n. 3, 372, 399; III 55 n. 3; IV 70 n. 3.

'Asár (works), I 407.

ʿAses-Báshi (Captain of the Watch), III 217 n. 1.

ʿAshiq, title given to a class of poets, V 46 n. 1.

ʿAshq-i haqíqi (real love), III 174 n. 2; IV 123 n. 1. See Love, Typal and Real.

ʿAshq-i mejází (typal love), III 174 n. 2; IV 123 n. 1. See Love, Typal and Real.

ʿAshúrá (10th of Muharrem), the, IV 112 n. 1.

'Asitána, name of Constantinople, III 214 n. 1.

'Asitána-i Saʿádet (The Threshold of Felicity), III 214 n. 1.

'Asmán u rismán, Persian phrase, IV 152 n. 1.

Asper = aqcha, I 262 n. 2.

'Asumání, name of a boot, III 295 n. 2.

'Asyáb (mill), V 48 n. 2.

Atles (satin), I 43 n. 2; IV 136 n. 1.

ʿAwálim-i Khamsa (The Five Worlds), I 54. See Worlds, the Five.

Aʿyán (Prototypes), I 410 n. 2.

Aʿyán-i Devlet (Grandees of the Empire), II 274 n. 2.

Aʿyán-i Sábita, (The Fixed Prototypes), I 55 n. 1. See Ideas, the Platonic.

Ayaq, III 186 n. 1.

'Ayna (mirror), V 30.

ʿAyn-i Tevhíd (The Eye of Unity), I 328 n. 1.

Chay, IV 68 n. 2.

Chekmek, IV 156 n. 3.

Chelebi, meaning of, I 139 n. 4.

Chelebi Efendi (title), I 151 n. 3, 422; IV 177 n. 1, 178, 212.

Chelebi Sultan (title), II 366.

Cherkh-i Atlas (The Fleckless Sphere), I 43. See Primum Mobile.

Cherkh-i A'zam (the Most Great Sphere), I 43. See Primum Mobile.

Chille, IV 156 n. 3.

جقندى, IV 170 n. 1.

Chörek, II 334 n. 12.

Dágh (sore), II 206 n. 2, 214 n. 4, 279 n. 5.

Dá'í (bedesman), *makhlas* of the poet Ahmed, I 259 n. 8.

Dakhíl, I 75 n. 1.

Dákhil, class of *muderris*, II 398.

Dákhil medreses, II 396.

Dánishmend, II 397.

Dár ú gír, III 19 n. 4.

Darisi bashine, IV 292 n. 2.

Dáriyye (mansion-poem), III 177.

Dár-ul-Hadís, a class of Muderris, II 399.

Dár-ul-Jelál (The Mansion of Glory), I 36 n. 1.

Dár-ul-Jihád (Seat of the holy war), I 397 n. 2.

Dár-us-Selám (The Abode of Peace), name of Baghdád, III 71.

Dár-us-Selám (The Mansion of Peace), one of the Eight Paradises, I 36 n. 1.

Dástán (legend), I 183, 270.

Dede (title), I 195 n. 3; IV 175 n. 1.

Defter-i A'mál (Register of Deeds), II 213 n. 7.

Defter Emini, the office of, IV 93.

Defterdár, the office of, I 428; II 25, 366; II 264; III 216 n. 4; IV 68, 93.

Defter-Kháne, IV 92.

Deñiz qulaghi, III 99 n. 2.

Der-i Devlet, name of Constantinople, III 214 n. 1.

Der-i Sa'ádet, name of Constantinople, III 214 n. 1.

Destár, IV 133 n. 1.

Deverán-i Vujúd (the Circle of Existence), I 52.

Devlet-i 'Aliyya, official title of the Ottoman State, III 207 n. 1.

Devlet-i Behiyya-i 'Irán, official title of the Persian State, III 207 n. 1.

Devshima, a species of conscription, III 117, 120.

Dibáje (Prologue), II 234.

Dik-i 'Arsh (The Cock of the Throne), II 333 n. 3.

Dín ve dunyásini yapmaq, II 320 n. 7.

Div-bend, title of King Tahmúras, III 360.

Diwán (Collection of Poems), I 85, 100, 102.

Hareket-i Khárij, class of Muderris, II 399.

Hasb-i Hál (Plaint), II 78 n. 3.

Hashish, II 340 n. 1; III 89 n. 1.

Hátif, the unseen, III 124.

Hátif-i Ján (Inward Monitor), I 313.

Hawá, the two meanings of, II 204 n. 3, 206 n. 1, 209 n. 2, 221 n. 11; III 157 n. 4.

Hawá-engíz, II 204 n. 3.

Hawá'i-Top (sky-cannon), II 239 n. 4.

Hayder (Lion), surname of the Caliph ʿAlí, III 289 n. 3; IV 123 n. 2; V 93 n. 3.

el-Hayy (the Living), a name of God, II 202 n. 3.

Hazf, name of a rhetorical figure, I 121.

Hazrát-i Khamsa (The Five Planes), I 55.

Hazret-i ʿAmá (Plane of the Nebulosity), I 55.

Hazret-i Ghayb-i Mutlaq (Plane of the Absolutely Invisible), I 55.

Heft Manzar (the Seven Pavilions), III 367.

Hekim Bashi (Chief Physician), II 399 n. 2.

Helwá-yi raqíb (rival's sweetmeat), II 108 n. 1.

Hemshíre-i sáqí-i sheng, III 269 n. 4.

Heyúlá (Matter), I 45.

Hezej, name of a metre, I 88 n. 1, 89, 107, 110, 309, 376; III 213.

Hezeliyyát (Facetiae), I 98.

Hiják-i núráni (veil of radiance), I 405 n. 2.

Hiják-i zulmáni (veil of darkness), I 405 n. 2.

Hijáz, name of a musical mode, III 150 n. 2.

Hijre (the Muhammedan era), I 98.

Hijv (Satire), I 98.

Hikáyet-i Munásib (Apposite Tale), II 145.

Hikmet-i ʿAmaliyye (Practical Philosophy), I 40.

Hikmet-i Nazariyye (Theoretic or Speculative Philosophy), I 39.

Hinna (henna), pronounced *qina* in Turkish, III 98 n. 1.

Hisáb-ul-Benán (Finger-Counting), I 104 n. 2. See *Parmaq Hisábi.*

Hiss-i Mushterek the (Common Sense), I 50.

Hubút, astrological term, I 328 n. 1.

Hu-hang, III 139 n. 1.

Hulúl (immanence of God in Man), I 382 n. 1.

Humá, the, I 331 n. 5 and 6; II 90 n. 1 and 2, 210 n. 3 221 n. 11; III 153 n. 3; IV 27 n. 2, 92 n. 1.

Huqqa-báz (juggler), II 38 n. 4.

Philosophy), II 396. See *Mu-tekellimín* and Scholastics.

ʿIlm-i Maʿání (Science of Significations), I 111; II 396.

ʿIlm-i Mantiq (Logic), I 40 n. 4; II 396.

ʿIlm-i Nahv (Syntax), II 396.

ʿIlm-i Reml (Geomancy), I 389 n. 1.

ʿIlm-i Riyází (Mathematics), I 40.

ʿIlm-i Sarf (Grammar), II 396.

ʿIlm-i Tabíʿí (Physics), I 40.

ʿIlm-i Taʿbír (the Science of Interpretation of Dreams), I 389 n. 1. See Dreams.

ʿIlm-i Tasavvuf (Súfiism, I 15. See Súfiism; Súfí; Mysticism; Mystics.

ʿIlm-i Tedbír-ul-Medíne (Politics), I 40.

ʿIlm-i Tedbír-ul-Menzil (Oeconomics), I 40.

ʿIlm-i Teressul, I 257.

ʿIlm-i Tevhíd (Knowledge of the Unity), I 166 n. 6, 304 n. 2, 328 n. 1.

ʿIlm-i Teʾvíl (Exegesis), II 397.

ʿIlm-i Yaqín (the Knowledge of Certainty), I 328 n. 1.

Iltizám (Supererogation), I 75 n. 1, 122.

Imále (Inclination), I 106; III 14, 15, 53, 143, 256.

Imám, meaning of, II 218 n. 1.

Imám = precentor, III 215 n. 4.

Imkán (Contingent Existence), I 42 n. 2. See Being, Contingent.

Iʿnát, name of a rhetorical figure, I 122.

Infiʿál (Passivity), I 41 n. 2.

Insán (Man), I 48.

Insán-i Kámil (the Perfect Man), I 52. See Man, the Perfect.

Ipsiz, IV 131 n. 2.

Iqtibás (Quotation), I 112.

Irádí (voluntary), I 44.

Irsád (Preparation), I 121.

Irsál-i Mesel (Proverbial Commission), I 114; III 329; IV 76.

Isfahán, name of a melody, IV 49 n. 3.

Ishtiqáq (Paronymy), I 120.

Ism-i Aʿzam (the Most Great Name), I 379 n. 2; III 56 n. 6. See Name, the Most Great; and God, the Most Great Name of.

Ism-i Rabb (the Name Sustainer), I 410 n. 3.

Ism-i Zát (the Name of Self), I 409 n. 1.

Ismidˉ (stibium), II 274 n. 1.

Istiʿáre (Trope), I 111 n. 1.

Izáfet (Persian genitive construction), III 81 n. 2.

Izáfet (Relation), I 41 n. 1.

ʿIzár (cheek), III 183 n. 4.

ʿIzzet (Excellence), IV 157 n. 2.

Kelime (the Muslim Confession of Faith), II 218 n. 4.

Kem (Quantity), I 41 n. 2.

Kemend, (lasso), II 114 n. 6.

Kendini oqut, IV 25 n. 1.

Kenez, (title) V 105 n. 1.

Kerake, IV 132 n. 4.

Keshf (unveilment), I 59, 327 n. 2.

Keshkúl, (begging-bowl), IV 173.

Kesre-i khafífa, III 212, 213 n. 1; IV 184 n. 1.

Kevn u Fesád (Generation and Corruption), I 47.

Keyf (Quality), I 41 n. 2.

Keyfiyyát (Qualities), I 47.

Keymus (chyme), IV 340 n. 2.

Kh'áb-i bí-ghaflet (sleep unoblivious), II 210 n. 2.

Kh'áb-i ghaflet (sleep oblivious), II 210 n. 2.

Khafíf, name of a metre, I 109, 305; II 144, 199 n. 3.

Khaftán Aghasi (Master of the Robes of Honour), IV 212.

Khalá (vacuum), I 44.

Khalíl (Intimate), II 253 n. 5.

Khalíl-ulláh (God's Intimate), title of Abraham, II 118 n. 2, 253 n. 5.

Khalláqu 'l-Ma'ání (Creator of Ideas), title of Kemál-ud-Dín of Isfahán, II 291 n. 2; III 51 n. 1.

Khalqiñ gözlerini boyardi, a Turkish idiom, I 300 n. 1.

14

Khán, meanings of, I 413 n. 2.

Khánim, title given to Turkish ladies, II 123 n. 1.

Kháqán, title of the Emperors of Tartary, II 115 n. 6; III 139 n. 1.

Khárchín, name of a metal, I 276.

Khárij (External), class of Muderris, II 398.

Khárij (External) medreses, II 396.

Kháss Hájib (Privy Councillor), I 71.

Khatíb (preacher), II 73 n. 6.

Khatt (writing *or* down), II 89 n. 5, 137 n. 1, 282 n. 2, 315 n. 7. See Down.

Khattí (Scriptory), I 119.

Khatt-i reyhání, a kind of handwriting, II 282 n. 2.

Khatt-i Yáqútí, a kind of handwriting, III 220 n. 2.

Khátún (Lady), II 123 n. 1.

Khawámis-i Suleymániyye, class of Muderris, II 399.

Khayál (Fantasy), I 50; II 36 n. 7, 208 n. 2; IV 172 n. 3. See Fantasy.

Khayfá, rhetorical figure, I 121.

Khayr-ul-'Al (the Best of Families), II 239 n. 3.

Khayr-ul-Besher (Best of Mankind), title of Muhammed, I 243 n. 1.

Khayr-ul-Enám (Best of

Mesnevís, I 101, 102, 107 sqq.

Metá (Time), I 41 n. 2.

Mevjúd (Actualised), I 407.

Mevlánâ, title, I 145 n. 1.

Mevlid, Mevlúd (Birthsong), I 232 n. 4, 233.

Mevlid-Kh̲án, I 238.

Mevlúd Jemᶜiyyeti (Birthsong Meeting), I 237.

Mevlúdji, I 238.

Mewálid-i Seláse (the Threefold Offspring), I 48.

Mihr, double meaning of, II 204 n. 1; III 97 n. 5.

Mihráb (prayer-niche), I 224 n. 1; II 35 n. 2, 210 n. 1, 249 n. 4, 252 n. 4, 283 n. 2; III 94 n. 1, 115 n. 2.

Mil (needle), II 274 n. 1.

Millet (the Nation), V 19.

Millí román (national novel), V 14.

Minder (cushion), III 189 n. 2.

Mintan, IV 131 n. 5.

Mír-i Mejlis (Master of the Feast), II 333 n. 2.

Miᶜráj (Ascension of the Prophet), I 77, 236, 366 n. 2; IV 19. See Muhammed, the Ascension of.

Misráᶜ, misraᶜ (Hemistich), I 79.

Misráᶜ-i 'Azáde (Independent Hemistich) I 79.

Mistar, an instrument for ruling paper, Il 241 n. 6, 342 n. 6.

Miyán (Middle), musical term, I 97.

Miyán-Kháne (Middle-House), I 97.

Muᶜád, I 116.

Muᶜammá (Enigma), I 100.

Muᶜarrif (mosque-chorister), II 368.

Muᶜashsher (Tensome), I 94; IV 122.

Mubálagha (Hyperbole), I 112.

Muderris (Principal), II 30, 395 sqq.; III 219.

Muderris (Principal), classes of, II 398 seq.

Muᵓesses rhyme, I 75 n. 1.

Mufred (Unit), I 79.

Muftí, II 353 n. 2.

Muftí, official dress of the, III 295 n. 2.

Muftí-us-Saqalayn (Muftí of the Two Ponderables), II 354.

Mughílán (acacia), IV 263 n. 1.

Muhaddid-ul-Jihát (Limiter of Directions), I 43 n. 3. See Primum Mobile.

Muharref (Altered), I 118.

Muharrem, the first month of the Muhammedan year, II 387 n. 1.

Muhmel (Unmarked), I 98.

Muhtáj (Dependent), I 42.

Muhtesib (censor of public morals), II 77 n. 2; III 59 n. 2.

Muᶜíd (Répétiteur), II 397.

Mujtes metre, I 109.

*Mutessa*ᶜ (Ninesome), I 94.

Mutevelli (administrator), II 46.

Muveshshah (Acrostic), I 124.

Muwassal, rhetorical figure, I 121.

*Muzári*ᶜ metre, I 109.

Muzdevij (Pairing), I 92—94; IV 235.

Nahs-i Asghar (the Lesser Infortune), II 125 n. 1.

Nahs-i Ekber (the Greater Infortune), II 125 n. 1.

Ná²ib (Deputy-judge), II 397.

Naqarát (Chorus), I 97.

Naqd-i Rewán, double meaning of, IV 126 n. 3.

Naqíb-ul-Eshráf (Dean of the Sherífs), II 399 n. 2; IV 351; V 107 n. 1.

Náqis (Defective), I 118.

Náqisat-ul-ᶜAql (Deficient in Reason), term applied to women, II 130 n. 1.

Naqqásh (miniaturist, etc.) II 98 n. 1.

Naqsh ber áb (a picture upon water), II 242 n. 5.

Nár (fire), symbolical meaning of, I 171 n. 2.

Nárgíl, IV 65 n. 3.

Nasb (Fixture), I 187 n. 2.

Nasíb (portion), II 108 n. 1.

Nasíb, meaning of in the Qastamuni dialect, II 108 n. 1.

Naᶜt (Hymn to the Prophet), I 101; III 319; IV 19, 216, 338; V 49 n. 2.

Nazíra (Parallel), I 99, 228.

Nazm, I 87.

Nebíd, nebíz, III 89 n. 2.

Nefs (lust), I 198 n. 1.

Nefs (the Psychic), I 42.

Nefs (self) contrasted with ᶜAql (reason), II 296 n. 2, 389 n. 1.

Nefs-i Emmáre (the Commanding Flesh), I 198 n. 1; IV 277 n. 3.

Nefs-i Evvel (the First Soul), I 42.

Nefs-i Haywániyye (the Soul Sensible), I 48, 198 n. 1.

Nefs-i Kull, (the Universal Soul), I 42.

Nefs-i Levwáme (the Upbraiding Flesh), I 198 n. 1.

Nefs-i Mutma²inne (the Pacified Flesh), I 198 n. 1.

Nefs-i Nátiqa (the Soul Reasonable), I 48.

Nefs-i Nebátiyye (the Soul Vegetable), I 48, 198 n. 1.

Nehávend (name of a melody) IV 49 n. 3.

Nehr-ul-ᶜAsí (the Rebel Stream), IV 147 n. 2.

Nejáshí, title, III 139 n. 1.

Nesíb (Exordium), I 84.

Nesím (Zephyr), I 370 n. 3.

Neskh, a kind of handwriting, I 420; IV 78 n. 2.

Nevbet (performance by a military band), II 248 n. 4.

Qadáyif, II 335 n. 6.

Qádi-ᶜAsker, See *Qázi-ᶜAsker*.

Qadin (Lady), II 123 n. 1.

Qádir (Able), a name of God, I 409 n. 1.

Qafes (Cage), name of a head-dress, IV 262 n. 4.

Qaftan a kind of robe, IV 131 n. 4.

Qalavi, a kind of head-dress, III 295 n. 2.

Qalb (Anagram), I 119.

Qalb-i Mustevi (Palindrome), I 119.

Qalem (Reed-pen), III 272 n. 3. See Reed-pen.

Qalem-dán (Pen-and-ink case), III 308 n. 4.

Qalender, I 357 n. 1, 385 n. 1 and 3.

Qalláb (hook, perch), IV 116 n. 3.

Qalyonji Odasi (Barracks of the men-of-war's men), IV 301 n. 3.

Qalyonjis (galleon-men), the, IV 301 n. 3.

Qan bichaq olmaq, idiomatic phrase, II 321 n. 4.

Qanáᶜat tashi (Stone of contentment), III 56 n. 1.

Qánún (Code of Laws), III 8.

Qara (Black), used as a sobriquet, II 138 n. 1.

Qara Bataq (Cormorant), name of a melody, III 346 n. 5.

Qara-qulluqji (Black Watchman), title, III 185 n. 5.

Qara yel (the black wind), II 120 n. 5.

Qasída (Purpose-Poem), I 83 sqq., 101, 102, 144.

Qasída-i Beháriyya (Spring Qasída), I 101.

Qasída-i Dáriyya (Mansional Purpose-Poem), III 177 n. 9.

Qasída-i Ráᵓiyya (R Qasída), I 101.

Qasrí (Compulsory), I 44.

Qavs-i Nuzúl (the Arc of Descent), I 52.

Qavs-i ᶜUrúj (the Arc of Ascent), I 52.

Qawwás, qawas, V 43 n. 2.

Qaysar (Caesar), I 259 n. 7; III 139 n. 1.

Qaysar-i Rúm (Caesar of Rome), I 149 n. 1.

Qázi-ᶜAsker (Army-Judge), II 24 n. 3, 394 seq., 398 seq.

Qázi-ul-Háját, a title of God, I 365 n. 6.

Qibla, I 361 n. 4; II 59 n. 2.

Qibla-náme, V 92 n. 5.

Qibla-numá, V 92 n. 5.

Qich levendi, IV 114 n. 2.

Qilij-Timari (Sword-Fief), III 216 n. 1.

Qina, the Turkish pronunciation of *hinna* (henna), III 98 n. 1.

Qitᶜa (Section), I 87.

Qiyám (standing up), III 150 n. 4.

Qiz naqshi (maidenly), II 131.

Great Blackness), mystical term, I 377 n. 1. See Dazzling Darkness and Light, the blackest.

Seyyid, title, I 343 ; II 390.

Sha'bán, the month of, IV 298 n. 2.

Sháh, title, 433 n. 2.

Sháh-Beyt (Couplet-Royal), I 81. See *Sheh-Beyt.*

Shahna-i Mejlis (Master of the Feast), II 333 n. 2.

Shah-suwár (Cavalier), IV 114 n. 2.

Shalwár (trousers), IV 131 n. 3.

Shalwárli shináver, IV 131 n. 3.

Shámi (Syrian), meaning 'dark', III 150 n. 2.

Shaqq (Cleavage), a mode of execution, II 279 n. 7.

Sharqi (Oriental) V 7.

Sharqi, the, a verse-form, I 96, 103; III 319 seq., 322; IV 8, 44 sqq., 211, 280 seq.

Sháyagán hoard, the, IV 262 n. 1.

Sheb-chirágh (Night-Lamp), a fabulous gem, I 291 n. 1; IV 145 n. 1.

Shefaq (After-glow), II 89 n. 1.

Sheftálú (peach), term for a kiss, II 371 n. 1; III 58 n. 3, 156 n. 2; IV 149 n. 1. See Kiss and Peach.

Sheh-Beyt (Couplet-Royal),

I 81; III 174 n. 4. See *Sháh-Beyt.*

Shehíd (Martyr), III 155 n. 3.

Shehirli, II 227 n. 2.

Shehnáma, books entitled, III 4.

Shehnámaji, the office of, III 4.

Shehnáz (Coquetry), name of a musical note, I 222 n. 5.

Shehr oghlani (City lad), II 227 n. 2.

Shehr-engíz (City-Thriller), the, II 232; III 55; IV 15, 121, 228.

Sheker-kuláhi (Sugar-cap), I 238.

Shekker Bayrámi (the Feast of Sweetmeats), IV 62 n. 4.

Shemse (Solar disc), II 60 n. 5.

Shemse-i zer-kár (gilt sun), II 341 n. 1.

Shemsí dulbend, name of a head-dress, II 242 n. 7.

شربنتلملك, a word used by tailors, IV 132 n. 2.

Sheref (Exaltation), an astrological term, I 328 n. 3.

Sheref (Honour), used as a proper name, IV 157 n. 2.

Sherif (descendant of the Prophet), IV 351.

Shewwál, the month of, IV 62 n. 4, 68 n. 1.

Sheykh-ul-Harem (the Elder of the Sanctuary), title, III 265 n. 3.

Tabí͑i (Natural), I 44.

Táj (Crown), name of a couplet, I 85; III 150 n. 6.

Tájik, I 186 n. 2.

Takhmís, name of a verse-form, I 92, 93; II 78 n. 3.

Tálib (Student), II 396.

Ta͑líq, a kind of handwriting, I 394 n. 2; III 220 n. 2; IV 78.

Ta͑miye (Enigmatizing), I 98.

Táq (Arch), II 59 n. 1, 60 n. 6, 62 n. 4, 63 n. 4. See Táq-i Kisrá.

Táq-i muqarnes, a kind of dome, IV 42 n. 2.

Táqche, II 60 n. 6.

Taqdís, name of a throne, II 315.

Taqsím, double meaning of, III 347 n. 5.

Tár, different meanings of, IV 132 n. 4.

Tard u ͑Aks (Epanodos), I 115.

Tárikh (Chronogram), I 87, 98. See Chronogram, Oriental.

Tárikh-i Támm (Perfect Chronogram), I 98.

Tariq-i Mebde (the Outward Track), I 52.

Tariq-i Ma͑ád (the Homeward Track), I 52.

Tazádd (Antithesis), I 112.

Tazmín (Quotation), I 113; II 49 n. 4.

Teblígh, a kind of Hyperbole, I 112 n. 1.

Tedvír (Epicycle), I 45 n. 1.

Tegellemek, a tailor's term, IV 131 n. 10.

Tejáhul-i ͑Arif (Feigned Ignorance), I 114; II 59 n. 3.

Tejellí (Epiphany), I 408 n. 1.

Tejnís (Homonymy), I 116, 212; II 77 n. 3, 221 n. 5; III 156 n. 5, 183 n. 4.

Tekye, I 357.

Tekfur, title, II 194 n. 2.

Tekur, title, II 194 n. 2.

Tel qirmaq, double meaning of, III 347 n. 4.

Telmí͑ a rhetorical figure, I 124.

Telmíh (Allusion), I 112.

Teng (closed), meaning '͑sorrowful', III 155 n. 5.

Ter (wet), II 101 n. 5.

Teráne, a name for the *Rubá͑i*, I 89.

Terbí͑, name of a verse-form, I 92, 93.

Ter-dámen (wet-skirted), II 101 n. 5.

Terjí͑-Bend, name of a verse-form, I 90, 91; III 64; V 65, 75, 86 sqq.

Terjí͑-Kháne, metrical term, I 90.

Terkíb-Bend, name of a verse-form, I 91, 94; III 90.

Terkíb-Kháne, metrical term, I 91.

Tersí͑ (Bejewelling), a rhetorical figure, I 123.

Umúr-i Milkiyya Náziri (Minister of Civil Affairs), IV 325 n. 1.

ʿUnnáb (the fruit of the jujube-tree), II 92 n. 2.

Urdi-bihisht, the Old Persian month of, III 265 n. 1.

ʿUrf, a kind of turban, III 295 n. 2.

ʿUshsháq (Lovers), a name for the Súfís, I 26 n. 1.

Ustá, title, IV 302 n. 8.

Usúl-i Qalem (the Bureaucratic style), IV 328. n. 1.

Vaqʿa-Nevís (Imperial Annalist), IV 67. See *Wáqiʿa-Nevís*.

Vebál (Fall), an astrological term, I 328 n. 3,

Vehm (Fancy), IV 172 n. 3.

Vesme, a kind of ointment, IV 101 n. 3.

Vesmelu (painted with indigo), III 98 n. 4.

Vezír (Minister), III 18 n. 2.

Viláyet (province), I 164.

Vujúb (Necessary Existence), I 42 n. 2.

Vujúd (Actuality), I 407, 408 n. 1.

Vujúd (All-comprising Existence), I 42 n. 2.

Vujúdiyye, a heretical sect, I 406.

Wájib-ul-Vujúd (Necessary), I 41.

Wáli, the office of, V 109 n. 7.

Wáqiʿa-Nevís (Imperial Annalist), IV 58. See *Vaqʿa-Nevís*.

Warsaghi, a kind of ballad, I 166 n. 5.

Wásita (Link), name of a couplet, I 90, 91, 94.

Watan (Fatherland), V 19.

Wazʿ (Situation), I 41 n. 2.

Yá ʿamú (O uncle), II 389 n. 2.

Yá Hú (Oh He!), IV 204 n. 3.

Yá Sin, name of a chapter of the Koran, V 38 n. 1.

Yagh qapani (Oil weigh-house), IV 301 n. 4.

Yashmaq, a veil worn by Turkish ladies, III 180 n. 1; IV 219 n. 1, 294 n. 2.

Yawuz (Grim), title of Sultan Selím I, II 257 n. 1.

Yazili elma (written apples), the, of Aspuzi, III 318 n. 4.

Yede tashi, a magic stone, II 120 n. 1.

Yel-qowan (wind-chaser), name of a bird, IV 277 n. 1.

Yeñicheri (Janissary), I 179 n. 1; II 76 n. 1. See Janissaries.

Yeñicheri Aghasi (General of the Janissaries), II 268 n. 2.

Yeshil toz (the green poplar), III 98 n. 4.

Yetishme, Yetishmesi (Mayst thou not grow up!) IV 294 n. 3.

15

INDEX IV.

SUBJECTS.

'Abbás, enigma on, I 100 n. 1.

'Abbásid Caliphs, black standards of the, II 213 n. 1.

'Abdulláh, used in naming slaves, II 93 n. 2.

Ablution, the canonical, II 218 n. 6.

Absorption in the Deity, I 59, 63.

Acrostic, the, I 124.

Adam, worshipped by the angels, IV 211 n. 1.

Admiral, the Grand, official dress of, III 295 n. 2.

Admiral, the Lord High, IV 47.

Adrianople, Treaty of, IV 306.

Aetiology, II 220 n. 4, 273 n. 5, 281 n. 5. See *Husn-i Taʿlíl.*

Ages of Man, the Seven, I 184.

Ahmed, the Light of, III 196 n. 3.

'Ajemí Oghlans, Corps of, III 118.

Alexander's Dyke, IV 103 n. 3.

Alexander, the Mirror of, I 284; II 339 n. 2.

'Alien', the, I 360 n. 7.

Alláh (God), I 181 n. 1, 379 n. 2, 409 n. 2.

Alláh, definition of, I 409 n. 2.

Almond, the, type of a beautiful eye, II 371 n. 2.

Alms, the public, II 89 n. 7.

Aloes-wood, the best variety of, III 32 n. 4.

Aloes-wood, perfume of, I 215 n. 1.

Alphabet, the Ottoman, I 98 n. 1.

Ambergris, the type of darkness, III 32 n. 2.

Amphibology, II 87 n. 3, 108 n. 1, 114 n. 9, 127 n. 4, 137 n. 1, 204 n. 1, 207 n. 2. See Word-plays, *'Ihám*, and *Tevriye.*

Anagram. See *Qalb.*

Angels, the, I 38. See *Melekút.*

Angels, the, called Heavenly Birds, IV 204 n. 1.

Angels, Recording, II 213 n. 7.

expression of bewilderment, I 331 n. 1.

Black Stone, the, I 38.

Blackness, the Most Great. See *Sewád-i A'zam*.

Blackness of face, typifying disgrace, IV 72 n. 6.

Blood, to take blood upon one's neck, IV 262 n. 5.

Blue and green, regarded as shades of one colour, I 151 n. 3; II 112 n. 7; III 31 n. 6, 98 n. 4.

Body, the, compared to a cage, I 190 n. 4.

Body, definition of, I 45 n. 3.

Books, the four, I 375 n. 2.

Books, want of reverence for, II 355 n. 2.

Bosom, the, compared to a sepulchre, IV 171 n. 2.

Bowl, the Elder of the, IV 205 n. 1.

Brazil-wood, II 213 n. 2, 254 n. 8.

Bread and salt rights, II 315 n. 6.

Breath of God, the, title of Jesus, III 214 n. 3.

Breath, holding of the, practised by dervishes, III 240 n. 3.

Breezes playing on water, likened to chains, II 242 n. 4.

Bride, the Spheral = the sky, II 60 n. 6.

Brides, the faces of, ornamented with gilt spangles, III 31 n. 3.

Bridge, the, of Hell, I 174 n. 2. See Sirát.

Bridle-fere, IV 49 n. 1.

Brocade, Venetian, II 255 n. 2.

Bud, a, compared to a goblet, IV 334 n. 1.

Bull, the, in Muhammedan cosmogony, I 39.

Burning Bush, the miracle of the, IV 104 n. 1; V 94 n. 7.

Buttons, alluding to a lady's breasts, III 97 n. 2.

Cadi, the office of, II 394 seq., 397 sqq.

Cadiasker, the office of, II 24 n. 3. See *Qází-'Asker*.

Caiques, the public, IV 44 n. 3.

Calf, the golden, V 89 n. 1.

Caliphs, the Orthodox. See *Khulefá-yi Ráshidín*.

Camels, unruly, II 110 n. 4.

Camphor, the type of anything white, III 16 n. 7, 32 n. 2.

Canaan, the Moon of, IV 265 n. 2.

Canopy surmounting the Sultan's throne, III 309 n. 6.

Caravan, the, of human individuals, I 193 n. 1.

Caravanseray, I 193 n. 1.

Carlowitz, the Peace of, III 332.

Carnelians of Yemen, II 89 n. 2 and 3; IV 216 n. 1.

East, I 330 n. 5, 360 n. 8; II
222 n. 5.

'Magian', use of, in Persian
and Turkish poetry, III 232
n. 4.

Magic, Muhammedan, III
175 n. 1.

Magic lantern, the. See *Fá-
nús-i Khayál*.

Magic rite, a, practised by
the Tartars, II 120 n. 1.

Man, the Microcosm, I 194
n. 1, 366 n. 7 and 8.

Man, the Perfect, II 284 n.
3. See *Insán-i Kámil*.

Mandoline, ears of the, II
342 n. 4.

Mantles, trimmed with
squirrel-fur, IV 355 n. 1.

Market, a 'hot' or 'warm',
III 67 n. 4.

Marriages, Muslim, IV 114
n. 4.

Mars, the Sphere of, II 373
n. 3.

Mastic, proverbial phrase in
connection with, IV 38 n. 1.
See *Saqiz*.

Mathematics, I 40 n. 3.

Matter, I 45 seq.

Meat, pieces of, compared
to prayer-rugs, II 335 n. 1.

Mejnún, Arabic poems as-
cribed to, II 178 n. 1.

Mekka pilgrims, the sandal
worn by the, IV 263 n. 1.

Melancholia, II 65 n. 2. See
Sevdá.

Mercury, the planet, III 147
n. 4.

Mercury, the Sphere of, II
111 n. 1.

Mercy to the Worlds, title
of Muhammed, II 217 n. 2.

Mermaid, the, V 40 n. 1.

Metal, a thin leaf of, placed
beneath precious stones, IV
286 n. 2.

Metaphysic, I 40 n. 3.

Metaphysical poets, the
English, I 28 n. 1.

Metonymy, I 111 n. 1. See
Kináye.

Metres, used in Ottoman
poetry, I 107 sqq.

Mevleví costume, the, I 423.

Mevleví orchestra, the, IV
176 n. 1.

Mevleví order of dervishes,
the, I 146, 149, 151, 195 n.
3, 421, 422; II 356 n. 1; III
61 n. 3, 186, 211, 219, 292,
297, 312; IV 80, 83, 124 n.
4, 125 n. 1. 137 n. 1, 159, 175
n. 1, 176 n. 3, 177 sqq., 203,
207, 212, 320 n. 3, 337.

Mevleví poets, I 411, 422
sqq.

Mevleví poets, biographical
work on the, IV 197.

Microcosm, the, I 62, 63 n.
1, 66, 187, 194 n. 1.

Mine, the; a type of gene-
rous wealth, III 149 n. 2.

Miracles. See Saints; Moon,
splitting of the.

ADDENDA TO INDEX.

The following words should be added to Index III.

Feylaqús, name of a wonderful stone, I 276.
Filúri (florin), II 26 n. 3.
Jubbe, IV 132 n. 5.

APPENDIX.

First lines of the Turkish Text of the Poems translated in Volume V.

[۴٥٩] حق تعالى عظمتِ عالمنكك پادشهى

[۴٦.] چقدى بر باغكك ايچندن يوله بر ياشلو حمار

[۴٩۱] اشى يوق بر گوزلى سودى بگندى گوكلم

[۴٩۲] ياپمه بر فيلسوف نامشهور

[۴٩۳] سزا در گوكلمه ايتسهم خيال صورتكك ارقام

[۴٩۴] گورن صاحبكك آراسندن يوزك پارلديسنى

[۴٩٥] زينتِ روضهء جنّت ايده حق عزّ وجل

[۴٩٦] وارلغم خالقمكك وارلغنه شاهد در

[۴٩٧] نه غم اوجوب وطنمدن بعيد دوشلدمسه

[۴٩٨] بو كارگاه صنع عجب درساخانه در

[۴٩٩] اقشام اولور گونش كدر شمدى برادن

[۴٧.] حبّذا نصرِ همايون بديع الاحوال

Printed by Printforce, United Kingdom